Phoenix Indian School

PHOENIX INDIAN SCHOOL
The Second Half-Century

Dorothy R. Parker

The University of Arizona Press
Tucson

The University of Arizona Press
www.uapress.arizona.edu

Printed in the United States of America
22   21   20   19   18   17   7   6   5   4   3   2

ISBN-13: 978-0-8165-1679-7 (paper)
ISBN-13: 978-0-8165-3579-8 (Century Collection paper)

Book design by Martha Shibata, General Services Administration,
San Francisco.

This history was produced under a Cooperative Agreement between
the National Park Service and Arizona State University, in partial
fulfillment of the 1988 Memorandum of Agreement among the
Department of the Interior, the Arizona State Historic Preservation
Officer, and the Advisory Council on Historic Preservation. The
statements, findings, and conclusions presented herein are solely
those of the Author and do not necessarily reflect the views of either
the National Park Service or the Department of the Interior.

Library of Congress Cataloging-in-Publication Data
Parker, Dorothy R. (Dorothy Ragon).
Phoenix Indian School : the second half-century / Dorothy R. Parker.
p.   cm.
Originally published: 1990.
Includes bibliographical references.
ISBN 0-8165-1679-0
1. Phoenix Indian School—History—20th century. 2. Indians
of North America—Education—Arizona. 3. Indians of North
America—Arizona—History—20th century. I. Title.
E97.6.P4P5736   1996
373.791'73—dc20   96-31381
CIP

British Library Cataloging-in-Publication Data
A catalogue record for this book is available from the British Library.

♾ This paper meets the requirements of ANSI/NISO Z39.48-1992
(Permanence of Paper).

CONTENTS

IN MEMORIAM
"I Have Spoken"
by Dollie Mae Lee Yazzie*

You know me well, you who have walked through my doors and roamed my grounds for many years. In the end, you left with a formal farewell, to go your way and live your lives as intended. I am PHOENIX INDIAN HIGH SCHOOL, the pride of many Native American tribes, the First Americans of our beloved land. I may be old in man-calculated years (ninety-nine, they say), but I could have lived another century or two without complaining of aches and pains, of dimming sight or failing memory.

On May 23, 1990, many of my former students returned to see me and their friends of years past. How joyous I felt as one by one they returned and walked again upon my trodden grounds. Seeing each familiar face brought back memories of wondrous fun-filled years and of events in the lives of these fine young men and women. I shed a tear for those no longer with us who could not be here. Do I feel an animate movement? A breeze of a different sort? Yes! Their spirits have walked upon the wind and joined us!

Traveling down memory lane is an experience I would not have traded for anything in this world. Many memories were a little painful, but the happy times far over-shadowed the sad. The happy times flicker by as faces reflect what each individual saw in his own private mental video of memories.

Many a brilliant mind was challenged in my classrooms by dedicated, hard-working teachers. Budding leaders became teachers, nurses, government officials, business men and women, tribal leaders, police officers, administrative assistants, who returned to their reservations and helped their respective tribes. There were others who

---

*Dollie Mae Yazzie (Navajo) was a student at the Phoenix Indian School during the 1950s, when Glenn Lundeen was superintendent. She sent her essay to him immediately after the final graduation ceremonies, and he suggested that it be included in this history. With her permission, it has been somewhat shortened and edited.

chose to live in cities and compete on equal grounds with people of all races. Sometimes they came out ahead of all the others! How proud I am! I had the cream of the crop!

The many activities on my campus made life interesting and full of spirit throughout those ninety-nine years. I recall our band who traveled to many places and marched in many parades. The Rose Bowl, no less, and winning a prize there! Basketball games, football games, the cheering, the heartbreak losses, all come back to me now.

Graduation nights were always a physical, almost unbearable, pain. I've had to push another group of fledgling graduates out of the security of my enfolding grounds to test their wings of knowledge for which I'd prepared them well. Tears were shed. Parents proudly sat in the audience as "Triumphant March" and "Pomp and Circumstance" echoed through the palm trees as the graduates marched into the old Oval. (In later years this event was held in Memorial Hall.)

On my campus, in the foyer of the Memorial Hall, you will see photographs of thirteen former students enrolled in the PHOENIX INDIAN HIGH SCHOOL HALL OF FAME. They are honored for their contributions to society and their fellow men as well as their Indian tribes. There were and are many more deserving of the same distinction.

In the Memorial Auditorium, where many enjoyed a romantic formal dance or a jumping sock-hop; where laughter echoed back and forth between the walls; where the solemn NATIVITY had the people of Phoenix jamming into the building for standing room only (although presented for three nights); where many a tear was shed at graduation; here we met once more at an alumni dance to recall moments of the past.

And now the music has died down, the lights are turned off for the last time. Now the campus is sleeping, never to be awakened by young voices laughing and talking again. Now the time has come to part, the time for weeping sadly and quietly. For this end is nothing like the times before. This is very final – the grand finale. Wherever you go I'll live in your memories. Let the memories we shared and lived be tucked away in the corners of your minds, to borrow now and then for a nostalgic trip into the past. This will prolong my life long after they have plowed my grounds and all that is left is a street with my name on it. My life will live on in each of you. §

ACKNOWLEDGMENTS

This work was conceived as one part of a three-part project under the auspices of the National Park Service to commemorate the closing of the Phoenix Indian School in 1990. One part of the project involved an archeological analysis of the campus to determine if significant prehistoric or historic archeological remains were present, and to recover important information held by those remains. The second part of the project included the architectural documentation and graphic recording of the school's historic buildings. The third part was to be a history of the school from about 1930 to its closing. Dr. Robert Trennert, professor of history at Arizona State University in Tempe, had previously published a history of the school from its founding in 1891 to 1935.

What follows is an account of school life from the years of the Great Depression until 1990. Rather than a formal narrative dealing with policy matters, however, I have attempted to write of the people and events that remain in the memories of some of the students, teachers, and administrators who spent some part of their lives there. To do this, I travelled across much of Arizona. Senior citizens in the Indian communities at Sacaton, Salt River, Ft. McDowell, White River, Sells, Clarkdale, and Parker invited me to lunch and shared their memories. For the most part, those memories were happy ones, but sometimes there were painful ones, as well. I want to take this opportunity to thank all those who welcomed me so graciously, and I dedicate this work to them and to the generations of boys and girls who at some time attended Phoenix Indian School.

Thanks are also in order for others who contributed generously. John Lewis and his staff at the Inter Tribal Council of Arizona were my first contact as I began my research, and they were interested throughout. Their wise counsel concerning the last years of the school was especially helpful. I am grateful to them, also, for letting me help at the school during the Open House prior to the final graduation. I will not forget those days.

Special thanks go, also, to Glenn Lundeen and his wife, who welcomed me into their home, shared their memorabilia, and provided wise counsel about their many years at Phoenix Indian School. Wade

Head, Bureau of Indian Affairs (BIA) area director in Phoenix during the 1950s, offered insight into policy matters. Beverly Queal, leader of the Special Navajo Program, provided insight into that adventure in mass education. At the school, principal Milford Sanderson, Jeanna Robinson who as senior class advisor put the last year book together, and Mark Wallig in the library, all helped me find information that I needed.

The story of *The Little Herder* series caught my interest, and I gained much from interviews with Lloyd Kiva New at his home in Santa Fe and with Robert W. Young, professor emeritus in linguistics at the University of New Mexico, Albuquerque.

Some archival material was still at the school, but much had become scattered. Pat Etter, archivist at the Arizona Collection at Arizona State University, aided my search for old year books, school newspapers, and other relevant publications. The local BIA office was holding records and ephemera for the National Archives, and Eva Cook and her supervisor, Gerald Shipman, patiently complied with my requests for this or that box of photos or scrapbooks. Suzanne Dewberry at the National Archives in Laguna Niguel, California, knew where to find pertinent records for the 1930s and 1940s. The National Archives and Record Center and the Smithsonian Institution Archeological Archives, both in Washington, D.C., also provided relevant material.

Finally I want to thank Jim Garrison, who helped with the photographs, Col. John Johnson at the Arizona National Guard Museum in Phoenix, who allowed me to borrow some of the museum's display for the last Open House, and Robert Trennert, who was always "there" when I needed his advice. While errors of omission and commission in the story are my own, the story itself belongs to all the people who so generously gave of their time to help put it together.

The following list contains the names of those people in various Indian communities of Arizona who contributed to this account of the Phoenix Indian School. They welcomed me into their midst, and my story of the school owes much to them.

Fort McDowell Indian Community: Martha Camacho, Philip Dorchester, Hiawatha Hood, Lola King, Georgianna Matuck, Irene McLevain, Annalita Paya, Edward "Bob" Shenah, Emma Shenah.

Salt River Indian Community: Ella Andrews, Evely Burns, Nora Harvey, Dean Jackson, Bernice Phillips, Josephine Manual,

Menson Senich, Annalita "Gates" Smith, Wenima Washington, Gussie Williams.

Colorado River Reservation: Ellsworth T. Charles, Priscilla Eswonia, Phyllis Laffoon, Josie Lomayesva, Violet Travis.

White Mountain Apache Tribe: Wesley Bonito, Vincent and Annie Dawahongva, Evalina Clay, Hinton Elesta, Sue Thompson.

Tohono O'odham, Sells: Virginia Domingo, Dorothy Francisco, Matilda Juan, Lamera Lewis, Angelita Maldonado, Lolita Manuel, Mary Miguel, Alice Narcho, Elsie Norris, Irene Rieno, Elizabeth Valisto.

Gila River Indian Community: Ruth Marietta Garcia, Henrietta Nelson, Rita Pancott, Mervin and Rose Ringlero, Jasper Stewart, Leona Thomas.

Camp Verde Indian Community: Naomi Halsted, Lucille Jackson, Priscilla Joshua, Flora Kinsey, Geraldine Larson, Harrington Turner, Annie Wathagoma.

The following people talked with me informally at various times and places: Earl G. Chico, "Cy" Johnson, Henry A. Ramon, Archie J. Russell.

Phoenix Indian School

INTRODUCTION

Nineteen proud young Indian students crossed the stage of Memorial Hall at the Phoenix Indian High School on May 24, 1990, to receive their high school diplomas. Along with their forty-one non-graduating school mates, they became the last of thousands of Indian boys and girls, young men and women, who had attended the Phoenix Indian School since its founding in 1891.[1] For ninety-nine years, Indian children in Arizona, as well as a few from tribes scattered across the American West, had come to Phoenix to learn the skills that would enable them to adapt to the white man's world that increasingly surrounded them. Not all of them graduated - some stayed for only a few months - but all were affected by the school in one way or another.

There were many non-Indians who said good riddance as the school bade farewell to that last class and closed its doors forever. Over the years, the government's boarding schools both on and off the reservations had come under increasing criticism, and the Phoenix Indian School had not been immune to those attacks. The boarding schools had acquired a poor public image, and recurring problems had led to periodic critiques such as the Meriam Report of 1928.[2] Robert Trennert, in his study of the Phoenix Indian School from its inception in 1891 to 1935, maintained that the Meriam Report caused changes in the internal structure of all the schools, subjected them to embarrassing publicity, altered their traditional ideas and programs, and threatened to close them altogether.[3] The entire boarding school concept was undergoing extensive review and revision when John Collier, one of the most vocal critics, became Commissioner of Indian Affairs in 1933. Collier decided that most of the boarding schools on the reservations should be replaced by day schools through the sixth grade, and off-reservation boarding schools should be closed as rapidly as possible.

Policy in Washington was one thing, however, and local school administration was another. Policy was always sifted through the screen of particular circumstances and was subject to local interpretations and applications. This present work, therefore, is an attempt to examine how just one of those off reservation boarding schools, the one in Phoenix, Arizona, fared during the Collier years and beyond. It is not the author's purpose, however, to present an analysis of government policy. It is, rather, to look at the Phoenix Indian School as it adapted to policy changes and to see how those changes affected the students, teachers, and administrators who spent some part of their lives there. The school could not avoid being touched by larger events in the world around it. The Meriam Report, followed by the Great Depression of the 1930s, World War II and the subsequent federal policy of termination, the impact of rising ethnic awareness and the advent of "red power," all inevitably left an imprint on the school. The students and staff at the Phoenix Indian School coped with those events in positive and negative ways until the school closed in 1990.

In order to understand the final months of Phoenix Indian High School, it might be helpful to examine briefly its origins. According to Robert Trennert, the people of Phoenix, in urging the establishment of the school in 1891, were not particularly interested in converting the Indians into their neighbors. While assimilation might have been the goal of federal Indian policy, that goal was not shared by the people of Phoenix. Their interest in having an Indian boarding school near town was based primarily on its providing an exploitable source of labor for the developing citrus and cotton industries. The outing system as it was practised at Carlisle Indian School in Pennsylvania was well-known, and it was thought that a similar system might be the answer to the local need for field workers. Thus, the peaceful and industrious Pima and Maricopa Indians living nearby were viewed as a potential source of cheap labor. They should be given just enough education to make them useful as an argicultural working class. [4]

There were other advantages, as well, in having the new Indian School in Phoenix. Such an institution would attract teachers, staff, and administrators who would be desirable citizens for the growing town. Their income would benefit the local economy, and the school itself would be an important consumer of local services. The school would also put Phoenix on the map. Carlisle was already famous – an Indian school in Phoenix would attract similar national interest. As Robert Trennert observed, Phoenix at the time "was dominated by a group of energetic boosters who envisioned a great commercial future for the Salt River Valley," and the school was viewed as a financial investment and as a promotional device that would attract future development.[5] When the federal government offered to pay $6,000 of the $9,000 purchase price for the Hatch Ranch, local businessmen willingly contributed the other $3,000.

This spirit of local boosterism was an important factor in keeping the school open for almost one hundred years, despite periodic talk of its closure from the 1930s on. When the school's band, its dance groups, and its National Guard unit performed for civic events, local businessmen were pleased to claim them as the city's own. When problems arose, as they sometimes did, the school was far enough away from town (three miles, at first) that it was possible to look the other way. The school, after all, was costing the city nothing. If its children got into trouble in town, they were taken back to the school, as local authorities recognized no responsibility for wards of the federal government. The Indians paid no property taxes; therefore they received no state or local services.

Inevitably, however, the time came when the venture was no longer cost effective, when the value of the land itself used in some other capacity appeared greater than the economic benefits accruing from the school. Phoenix was expanding, and plans existed for high-rise buildings extending north along the Central Avenue Corridor, which included a large portion of campus real estate. In 1954, after Phoenix included the school site within the city limits, the federal government sold the northwest corner of the campus for a motel. It also declared the southeast corner of the campus to be surplus property and gave it to the Veterans Administration for a hospital. The school, whose original 160 acres were at one time in the country, now sat on 105 acres of prime real estate surrounded by city development. Urban planners were eager to have access to those remaining acres.

Robert Trennert has chronicled the growth of the school to 1935, when a sense of impending change was felt by most of those involved with Indian education. John B. Brown, Superintendent at Phoenix Indian School since 1915, had resisted those changes and refused to recognize their inevitability. Carl H. Skinner, who replaced Brown in 1931, was more open to a modernization of the traditional boarding school structure. From 1931 on, the Phoenix Indian School band no longer played Souza marches as the students filed into the dining hall for meals. Students were no longer required to wear uniforms, nor were they organized into marching cadres for daily drill. Under the guidance of Carl Skinner, a new day was dawning at the Phoenix Indian School.

1

A New Deal for the Phoenix Indian School

During the first years of John Collier's administration as Commissioner of Indian Affairs, there was considerable discussion about closing the Phoenix Indian School. Thanks to Arizona's Senator Carl Hayden, however, Collier finally realized that there was simply no educational alternative for older Indian children in Arizona. They would be unable to continue their education unless and until high schools were built on the reservations, and that possibility was years away. Collier was forced to accept the reality of Hayden's argument, and the school remained open, at least for the moment.

Nevertheless, the lower grades at the school were dropped temporarily, and enrollment, which had reached 950 in 1928, fell to 500 in 1935 and to 425 in 1936. The major cause of this decrease was the successful completion of a number of day-schools on the reservations, which enabled younger children to remain at home during their first years of school. While the day school program was far from an unqualified success (the lack of adequate roads and huge distances proved to be insurmountable obstacles in some areas), it did relieve the overcrowded conditions in the boarding schools that had caused some of the problems noted in the highly critical Meriam Report. Phoenix Indian School now accepted students primarily for the upper grades, although a small number of younger children from broken or unstable homes were admitted, as well.

Many of the youngsters who came to Phoenix in the 1930s had lived in the relative isolation of Arizona's mountains or deserts, and for them boarding school life was a totally new and often frightening experience. Speaking a foreign language, staying in a dormitory, sleeping on a bed, in a room with thirty or forty other children, eating on a regular schedule, learning "mine" and "thine" in a world obsessed with private ownership – the school environment could be and sometimes was traumatic. To ease the "transplant shock," a young child was often paired with an older student from the same tribe until the youngster became adjusted to the daily routine. While a few children who ran away never returned, others did come back, frequently at the insistence of a parent or grandparent who had learned the importance of schooling in his or her own life. By the 1930s, the industrial arts and homemaking classes were often taught by Indians, and former students assisted as aides or matrons in the dormitories, as well. The presence of reassuring older students and adults offered a measure of comfort during their first difficult weeks. Undoubtedly there were some students for whom the school was an unhappy experience, but most have recalled Phoenix Indian School as a place where doors were opened to opportunities in the world beyond the reservations.

The most immediate recollection of senior citizens who were children at the school in the early 1930s was the end of the militaristic discipline that had ordered daily life from the school's beginning. A system of merits and demerits granting or restricting a variety of privileges replaced promotion through the organized ranks as a way of recognizing good behavior. Tardiness and/or absence were some of the lesser infractions that drew demerits, while lying, stealing, drinking, and gambling were graver offenses. Since the students were responsible for the routine policing of the buildings and grounds, demerits meant extra time on maintenance detail as well as a loss of privileges. Cleaning the bathrooms was a common duty imposed at such times. Merits, on the other hand, were awarded for the lack of demerits, and those with merits became the leaders of student activities. Corporal punishment became much less severe than it had been previously and was frowned upon as policy. [1] It never completely disappeared, however, as such punishment was considered a deterrent to future misconduct by the other students.

Even without military-style discipline, however, school life remained strictly ordered. Days began with the shrill blast of the steam whistle from the boiler room, a blast that could be heard far beyond the campus itself and was sometimes the subject of irate complaints from nearby residents. Students made their beds in the prescribed fashion, arranged their clothes in a precise manner, washed their hands before meals, lined up to enter the dining hall, and ate with knives and forks. Shoes and fingernails were inspected regularly and symptoms of illness were noted promptly, as contagious diseases could spread like wildfire through the usually crowded dormitories. Students who appeared ill were sent to the school hospital. If they showed signs of tuberculosis, and some did, they were assigned to the school's sanitorium and continued their studies there. [2]

The operative word in student life was discipline, administered not only as punishment but to teach proper behavior according to a generally accepted definition of propriety. With two or three hundred students housed in a single building, most of whom had never before lived in a social group larger than an extended family, and with only two or three matrons and aides in charge, disciplined habits and behavior were essential to the school's communal life and were taught from the child's first days at the school.

Despite such chronic overcrowding, persistent lack of funds, and the difficulty of coping with the Washington bureaucracy, faculty and staff at Phoenix Indian School generally found their work significant and fulfilling. They became surrogate parents for many of the children, especially the younger ones, and during the summer many teachers took advantage of the opportunity to visit the children's homes. As the children returned to school in the fall, there were happy reunions. While it is true that teachers and staff embraced the prevailing assimilationist goals of the white society that employed them, a great many, if not all, were warm, caring people who were genuinely fond of the children.

The education offered to Indian children at all government schools, including Phoenix, had from the beginning reflected the American public's belief in assimilation, as well as its general lack of interest in Indian languages, culture, and religion. The melting pot, not cultural pluralism, was the goal of the educational process. At the same time, the melting pot concept as applied to minorities was itself limited by class and gender. Although there were exceptions, Indian children were considered incapable of benefiting from a college education. Boys were encouraged to become farmers or to learn skilled trades, not to become doctors or lawyers, while girls were taught homemaking skills. Both the academic and the vocational programs were oriented accordingly.[3]

During the depression years, however, the emphasis was on subsistence farming on the reservation because there were no opportunities for work in the outside labor market. Girls in general were expected to become wives and mothers, and Indian girls were no exception. When the labor market opened up during and after WWII and almost any skilled person could find work, the emphasis on farming lessened, but throughout this period, girls had far fewer opportunities than boys. Although their limited horizons gradually broadened, their schooling beyond the most basic academic skills still revolved around various aspects of homemaking. They learned to sew, to prepare healthy meals, and to observe basic practices of good hygiene for themselves and their families. This is not to say that these things were not useful, only that the girls' horizons were limited to them. The only employment open to them was in domestic service. This, too, however, would begin to change with time.

Many student activities dating from the earlier period of the school were unaffected by the changes that were taking place at the policy level. The Phoenix Indian School Band, for instance, which had achieved a degree of fame in the City of Phoenix and in the world beyond, continued to march with precision, although its services were no longer required as part of the daily routine. Under its first director, a German bandmaster trained in the old school, it had given many public concerts before its appearance at the Saint Louis World's Fair in 1904. The band had helped celebrate the dedication of Roosevelt Dam in 1911 and Arizona's admission to statehood in 1912, and it entertained the visitors at the dedication of Coolidge Dam in 1930. Through the years it had been called upon to play for visiting dignitaries, for civic events and funerals of important people, for parades and community dances.

In the 1920s and 1930s, the Indian School Band had also developed a tradition of presenting regular Sunday afternoon concerts for the citizens of Phoenix, and old-timers like Senator Barry Goldwater have recalled visiting the school to hear those concerts. During the years when uniformed students practised disciplined drill formations, the long parade ground in front of the dormitory and classroom buildings had been the site of public displays and activities. Now, however, such occasions were more apt to take place in the large oval space behind the Administration Building, where a bandstand to accommodate the musicians had been built in front of the flagpole. Double rows of stately palm trees converged at the bandstand, while rows of chairs on the grass in front provided seating for the guests. Several generations of Indian School graduates received their diplomas in that lovely park-like setting known as the Oval.

While the primary emphasis at the school was on training in the so-called industrial arts, the instructional program through the years also focused on language skills. Language was understood as the basic conveyor of culture, and since the purpose of all Indian education was to replace one culture with another, the children's use of their own

language was severely frowned upon and subject to demerits. After the
new students became somewhat acclimated to their new life, beds in the
dormitories were reassigned to avoid placing children from the same
tribe next to each other, thus forcing them to use English as their
common language. By the mid-1940s, most of the children who came to
the Phoenix Indian School had attended day school on the reservation
and could speak at least minimal English. Also, from the 1940s, rigid
enforcement of the English-only rule was a thing of the past. Nevertheless, reading, writing, and public speaking were essential skills in
relating to the non-Indian world, and they remained the most essential
part of the curriculum throughout the student's years at school.

Students practised their language and social skills primarily
through the increasingly democratic organization of their dormitories
and through a variety of weekly clubs and societies that encouraged
group participation at all grade levels. Prominent in the 1930s were
literary societies for both boys and girls that encouraged oral presen-
tations before a group of peers. Home economics clubs, Boy Scouts and
Campfire Girls, the Indian School Band and several choral groups, a
variety of athletic teams and the Lettermen's Club, religious organizations for both Protestants and Catholics, a National Guard Unit, and
an Indian dance group – these were some of the groups that formed from
time to time. All children were required to belong to at least one of these
organizations, and many students claimed membership in several.

The school was still relatively isolated in the 1930s and television
was unheard of, so the clubs provided a variety of activities that accom-
modated the developing interests of the students and occupied their free
time. The clubs were generally organized by age group, the seniors being
grades nine through twelve, the intermediates grades six through eight,
and the juniors grades three through five. Boys and girls had separate
clubs; as a practical matter, the various activities provided a relatively
effective means for keeping boys and girls apart.

Strict segregation of boys and girls was an accepted aspect of boarding school life and was enforced more rigidly perhaps than any other
general rule at this time. Protestant sexual mores were considered one of
the most important aspects of the child's indoctrination. Couple relationships were frowned upon and strictly monitored. In fact, a big project
during the summer of 1937 "was to erect barriers in the steam tunnels so
the boys could not tour the campus by the underground route. There had

been many excursions to Casa Saguaro (the girls' dormitory) and into other parts of the campus by that route during the winter."[4] Social clubs and steam tunnel barriers were part of the school's strategy in dealing with this aspect of student life.

The Boy Scout troops at the Indian School (at one time there were three of them, Troops 5, 25, and 26, but Troop 26 later moved to the new day-school at Salt River) provided an additional all-male activity, as well as another important bridge between the students and the outside community. As part of the Roosevelt Council, Boy Scouts of America, boys from the Indian school participated in a variety of scouting events with other Phoenix area Scouts. One boy from the school was believed to be the first Indian boy in the United States to achieve Eagle Scout rank, at least according to the local newpaper. Scouts from the school eagerly anticipated their overnight visits to the Heard Scout Pueblo, which had been donated to the Roosevelt Council in memory of Dwight Bancroft Heard in 1930. Dwight Heard had been an ardent supporter of scouting, and his gift, just nine miles from downtown Phoenix and adjacent to Hieroglyphic Canyon, provided the Scouts with access to remnants of the ancient Hohokam cultures of the Salt River Valley. The Indian School band had performed at the Scout Pueblo's dedication as part of the celebration of the twentieth anniversary of Scouting in America, and generations of Indian boys from the school participated in various activities there.

One wonders, however, about the impact of scouting in general, and the Heard Scout Pueblo in particular, on the boys from the Indian School. Here was a totally modern facility that was built as an Indian pueblo. It was decorated throughout with Indian art and Indian motifs, and its staff included a Director of Indian Lore. Did the boys from the Indian School ever see themselves in this setting as somehow different from the non-Indian boys they met there? Was it ever pointed out to them that those traditions and that architecture were originally theirs? (There is an old photograph in the files, probably from the 1920s, showing Scouts from the Indian School demonstrating how to make fire with "fire drills," Indian style!) The Boy Scout movement generally presented to its members the image of a generic Indian, while the reality for Native Americans has always been their tribal identity. It is difficult to say just what happened to that identity when the Indian boys mixed with non-Indian Boy Scouts, or when children from various tribes mingled at the school. The records, of course, are mute on this question, but they leave us wondering. Almost as visible to the Phoenix community as the band was an Indian dance group, which began as a Boy Scout activity in 1932. Its existence was something of an anomaly, as the Indian schools up to this time had discouraged the continuation of Indian cultural practices. Dances had been frowned upon because most of them were performed on the reservations as part of religious ceremonies. But the public was interested in seeing them, so the Boy Scout troops at the school were permitted to organize a dance group. Depending on the background of the student members, the group performed Apache, Navajo, Hopi, and other tribal dances. The dance group later became a separate activity open to all interested boys, not just Boy Scouts.

Major support for the dance group came from the Phoenix Dons, a civic organization that frequently sponsored the boys' public performances. For some years the dancers were a traditional part of the Dons' annual weekend event called "The Lost Dutchman Gold Trek," in the Superstition Mountains east of Phoenix. As a rule, the dance group charged admission for public performances, and the money earned was used to pay for the ceremonial clothing the boys created from models they brought from home. Like the band, the dance group provided high visibility for the Phoenix Indian School, and its performance at the Arizona State Fair became one of the fair's major attractions.

The expertise of young Indian dancers at the Phoenix school attracted the attention of Paul Coze, a noted French artist, ethnographer, and writer, who had been one of the founders of the Boy Scout movement in France. In 1939, Coze visited the school and wrote a ballet-drama for the dancers titled "The Desert Way." The story involved four boys, Hopi, Navajo, Apache, and Hualapai, who were sent by the Sun Father to search for Beauty. Each boy had a series of adventures that were highlighted in the drama by his people's traditional dances, which were performed with a drum accompaniment. Sets for the production were designed by Hopi student Charles Loloma, under the direction of the Cherokee artist Lloyd New, who had just been appointed as the school's new art instructor. Another of the school's teachers, Ira Grinell, Pottawatomi, was the narrator. Coze's drama was so successful at the school that several repeat performances were given for the Phoenix community. [5]

Although all the children at Phoenix Indian School were Indian, their identities were essentially tribal, and some of the tribes represented, the Pima and Apache, for instance, had been traditional enemies. Small children would perhaps not have been too much aware of this, but the older children certainly knew of their people's history. The school tried very hard to play down tribal differences, and there seems to have been no particular problem, but as with any group of children there were those who were "in" and those who were "out," and sometimes it was a question of tribal identity. One girl recalled that she had had a good friend from another tribe in the dorm, but neither would acknowledge the other when they were outside.

Many educators at the time believed that teamwork, especially in athletics, was a particularly effective way to deal with tribal rivalries, and team sports were encouraged. But on some occasions, tribalism carried the day, even on the playing field. It was difficult, for instance, to make linemen on the football team, who might be of a given tribe, understand the need to cooperate in helping their backs, who were from a different tribe, avoid the tackles of the opposing team in order to advance the ball. Teams or tribes – sometimes it was hard to tell which side the boys were on.

The Boy Scout troops at Phoenix Indian School were indicative of on-going efforts to assimilate Indians into mainstream American life, despite Collier's interest in promoting cultural pluralism. Another such effort was the continuing influence exercised by Christian churches, both Catholic and Protestant. Early Spanish missionaries had converted some southern Arizona groups to Catholicism, and Presbyterians and other Protestant denominations also had well-established congregations in Arizona's various Indian communities.

Students from those areas who expressed a continuing interest in Christianity were encouraged to join a non-denominational Protestant club or the Catholic Holy Names Society. While active proselytizing was no longer allowed in the boarding schools as it had been previously, ministers and priests at times held services at the school or arranged for students to attend a church in town. Sometimes members of various congregations would come by the school and pick the students up on Sunday morning or evening. Although attendance at church was not required, it was certainly encouraged; peer pressure as much as anything else accounted for many students' participation.

One active religious body connected for years with Phoenix Indian
School was Cook Christian Training School, which was located in the
immediate vicinity. Presbyterians had established the school in 1910 as
a training center for young Indians who planned to return to their
reservations as lay missionaries. By 1940, the school received its
financial support from the Home Missions Council representing twenty-
eight Protestant churches, and it was non-denominational. Dr. George
Logie, one of the early administrators at Cook Christian, directed
religious education at Phoenix Indian School for almost thirty years, and
he arranged for his students to conduct Bible study classes there on a
regular basis. While the Catholics were not terribly interested in holding
religious education classes at the school, they recognized the attraction
of the classes offered by the Cook Christian School people, so they, too,
began Sunday morning instruction.

One of the changes in educational policy advocated by John Collier
was a greater recognition of specific tribal traditions. Although various
Christian churches had fought against religious practices such as tribal
dances being allowed at the off-reservation schools, the curriculum
began to reflect Collier's interest in traditional lifeways. Students from
various tribes prepared exhibits and material on their own tribes for use
in class, and tribal officials visiting Phoenix were invited as guests, thus
reinforcing the students' tribal identities. As on the playing fields, however, cross-cultural education sometimes ran into unexpected problems.
In one instance, an attempted reenactment of a traditional Hopi wedding
proved difficult because the young couple who traditionally would have
wound their hair together to symbolize their union had such short hair
that it was impossible to perform this part of the ceremony!

Despite such occasional problems, the athletic program continued
to promote inter tribal cooperation, and it was a very important part of
the school curriculum in the 1930s. But competitive sports were for the
most part restricted to the boys; girls participated by providing moral
support and making team uniforms in their sewing classes. The premier
sport was football. In 1935, 333 boys participated to some degree in one
of five levels of play. The first and second varsity team members were
boys who were not older than twenty years of age, while the Panthers, a
junior varsity, were somewhat younger. The Shorties weighed under 130
pounds, while Papooses were the smallest and youngest boys. There was
also a group called the ineligibles, young men twenty-one and older, who

occasionally played alumni groups or similar teams from other Indian schools.

But athletic competition was not always between teams of equal size. The Indian schools had trouble finding teams willing to play against them, as the Indian students were often older and bigger than public school students at the same grade level. In 1933, for instance, the Phoenix Indian School football team lost only one game, and that by a score of 2 to 0. They scored a total of 244 points against 14 for their opponents that year.

Nevertheless, intense rivalry soon developed between Phoenix Indian School and two other schools, Phoenix Union High School and Sherman Indian School in Riverside, California. Phoenix Indian School played its first game against Sherman in 1924 and lost, 18 to 0, thus beginning a competitive tradition that lasted until 1939. The tradition was not of Sherman winning, as the two schools were relatively evenly matched, but of the exchange of a trophy called "Sally's Goat." The first mention of this trophy appeared in the Phoenix school newspaper, the Native American, after that first game. According to the report, "Sherman football players claim to have captured a certain small animal belonging to a former Sherman employee now serving as head matron at Phoenix School."[6] "Sally's Goat" was a stuffed toy four or five inches high dressed in a coat of the winning school's colors. The trophy was named for Miss Sally Taylor, a dorm matron who had moved to the Phoenix school from Sherman in January 1924. Miss Taylor probably brought "Sally's Goat" from Sherman, as competition between the two schools began the fall after she arrived. According to the school newspaper, "the said animal is the one commonly used in the initiation of secret societies" at Sherman.[7]

All the students were obviously fond of Miss Taylor, who enjoyed the competition between the two schools and often chaperoned the Phoenix team when it travelled to Riverside. More than once she was the honored guest at the school's annual football banquet, and in 1934 a group of former students, girls working in Phoenix, honored her with a party at the local YWCA on Mother's Day. Her long-fringed leather jacket, however, was a source of amusement for years. She apparently walked with a long swinging stride that exaggerated the movement of the fringe, and the students delighted in mimicking her. Affectionately, they called her "Buffalo Bill," behind her back, of course.

Another popular sport in the school's athletic program, beginning in 1929, was boxing. The Indian School boxing team produced several champions. In 1933, the boys travelled to San Francisco for an inter-scholastic regional meet, and a student named Johnnie Martin, who boxed as a flyweight, won special accolades. One of the California coaches wrote to Dick Brenton, the school's boxing coach, "I have never, in all my experience, seen an amateur come back after two hard knock-downs and make such an uphill fight and win, as he did. . . You seldom ever see such gameness as that Indian boy has." [8]

Basketball was one of the few competitive sports played by both boys and girls, with the girls' varsity playing against a similar varsity team from Sherman. Less formally the girls also played volleyball, baseball, and a game they called "hit pin baseball". An intramural soccer competition, between classes and even between literary societies, involved almost every girl at the school. Boys of all ages were equally active in baseball. Despite its success, the athletic program at Phoenix Indian School became a casualty of the falling enrollment, increased budget cuts, and another change of school administrators. Sharon Mote, who replaced Carl H. Skinner in 1937, wanted to deemphasize sports and place more emphasis on the school's academic and vocational programs. He felt that the athletic program had been over-extended, causing the players undue fatigue and significant loss of classroom time. Mote therefore eliminated the boxing and wrestling teams, and he reduced the football schedule to no more than two games a week, although the annual football competition with Sherman continued until 1940. "Sally's Goat" disappeared after that last game – perhaps it stayed at Sherman.

As another part of Mote's reorganization of the athletic program, more games were played closer to home, with local schools. Mote applied for membership in the Arizona Interscholastic Association at this time, and agreed to field teams according to the association's rules. The main difficulty in obtaining that membership was providing proof of the students' ages. Students were required to be less than twenty-one years of age to play in the association, and many of the Indian students had no birth certificates. Because of this, the school was denied full participation in the association for a number of years. Nevertheless, it adhered to the association's rules and refused to play any team that did not follow them.

Life at Phoenix Indian School during the 1930s was much more than fun and games, of course. During this period the curriculum of the school continued to focus on vocational rather than on academic education. The school was originally called an industrial training school, and its program for the most part centered on providing the students with opportunities to develop skills that would enable them to hold meaningful jobs outside the reservations. Training in a variety of trades was offered. During the seventh and eighth grades, boys spent several weeks or months testing different vocational areas. Later they were encouraged to choose one of several specialty trades where they would further develop their skills. Masonry, carpentry, painting, plumbing, and electrical work were among the various construction trades taught. Boys could also study auto mechanics, shoe making, tailoring, baking (under the watchful eye of Mr. Kilroy, the school's baker in the 1930s), or various aspects of agriculture and animal husbandry. Academic courses were designed to relate the more abstract academic skills to the various kinds of vocational work.

But a few students, both boys and girls, excelled in their studies, and those students were encouraged to continue their education. A number of them stayed at the school as resident graduates while they attended Phoenix Union High School, Phoenix City College, the Teachers Training College (later Arizona State University) in Tempe, or a local business school. They worked for their room and board as assistant matrons in the dorms or as assistants in the vocational programs. Tuition loans were available through the Bureau of Indian Affairs, and the school's staff helped the students cope with the required paper work in applying. These older students, with a different goal for their lives, provided the younger ones with a vision of other possibilities for the future, although the number of Indian students who successfully completed four years of college remained very low.

While the curriculum at Phoenix continued to offer vocational training, it also reflected the times. During the depression years there were few jobs available, and the school's agricultural program reflected that reality. Boys could still choose to concentrate on such skills as carpentry, masonry, and tailoring, but an expanded agriculture program was also available if they chose to return to the reservation. The school's farming operation, producing most of the fresh meat, milk, and garden produce consumed on the campus, instructed the students in large-scale production. During the Depression the school raised hogs, turkeys, and chickens, grew cotton, and ran a canning operation.

For the first time, girls were also admitted to portions of the agriculture program, and they responded enthusiastically. A Rural Home Training Program organized by Eleanor Palimo, a recent Papago graduate, revitalized an old tradition by providing senior girls with an opportunity to live in practice cottages where they "kept house" in conditions similar to those of wage-earning families in town. They also raised chickens and maintained a kitchen garden. The practice cottages were built by boys in the various construction programs. Some of the boys who were more advanced in agriculture, and some recent graduates as well, enrolled in another program called Subsistence Homestead Enterprises. They, too, were provided with a small cottage on campus to live in and enough acreage for a subsistence farm, which they ran under the supervision of the agricultural and home economics staff. As the girls were learning agricultural skills, the boys learned how to buy and prepare their own food, care for their clothes, and maintain their homes. A growing demand for these programs witnessed to their effectiveness in meeting student needs. [9]

The instructors for these various programs displayed an admirable flexibility. A number of them were themselves Indians, and they were able to adapt the students' needs to the demands of their home environment as well as to the school program. While a relatively small number of boys and girls were able to take full advantage of these innovations, most of the students gained at least a working knowledge of modern agricultural and homemaking skills that, hopefully, they could use wherever they lived.

In addition to their various training programs, older students at Phoenix Indian School, as at all the government boarding schools, were involved in what was known as the outing system. This system, which had been the subject of earlier criticism as unadulterated exploitation of cheap student labor, was continued through the 1930s and 1940s, but its structure by that time, at least at Phoenix Indian School, had been considerably modified.

In practice the outing system permitted the students to hire themselves out to the community for house work, gardening chores, seasonal farming, and in some instances practical on-the-job training. While in the 1930s the system may still have had occasional unfortunate episodes, it also provided useful lessons and helped establish acceptable work habits. Most of the students had had little experience either with regular work or with a cash income, and for the first time in their lives they learned about working for wages. There is no question about the wages being low, but during the Depression wages were low everywhere. The school maintained close supervision over working conditions and withdrew the child if those conditions were less than satisfactory. Many students became regular Saturday employees, and close relationships not infrequently developed between the student and the employer.

The most constructive change in the outing system occurred when students themselves gained some control over their labor. They could refuse to be involved at all, or they could refuse to work for a particular person. Given the choice, most of the students wanted to work. Their income offered them the freedom to buy candy and soda pop from Bill's Pantry, just across Indian School Road from the entrance to the school, or to go to a Sunday movie in town, with money they themselves had earned. Developing motivation for wage work and for earning and saving money, the essence of the American work ethic, was one of the primary goals in the education of the children, and the outing system at that time and place generally played a significant role in developing constructive work habits.

The boys and girls at the Indian School were not, as a rule, consigned to a summer outing program at this time. Most of the children went home for the summer, and this was encouraged by the new government policies. Some students, however, chose to work during summer vacation. They stayed at the school and paid a nominal sum for board and room, or lived with their employers, or roomed at the Phoenix YMCA or YWCA to shorten the commute to their jobs. In the summer of 1934, a number of girls found housekeeping jobs in the Prescott area, where they organized informally and met as a kind of literary club like the ones at school. That same year, sixty boys hired out to help build the Salt River Day School. They each earned five dollars a week, a considerable amount for most of them. Out of that they paid for room and board at the school and for their bus transportation to the work site each day. The Salt River School became a show place for student training in the construction trades.

As a public institution, Phoenix Indian School made a number of adaptations to depressed economic conditions during the 1930s. Under

Collier's leadership, the BIA called for greater diversification of school activities into Indian communities, and this took shape in several ways through the school. The Civilian Conservation Corps (CCC), the most popular of all the Roosevelt administration's relief programs, had an Indian branch that operated quite successfully in the Southwest. Called the CCC-ID, it established a unit at Phoenix Indian School, enrolling recent graduates who were unable to find employment elsewhere. Details of the arrangement between the school and the government indicate that $2,000 was provided in 1938 and $3,500 in 1939 to cover the school's cost of maintaining the program. [10]

There were lots of opportunities for CCC-type work at the school, especially since previous budget cuts had caused the physical plant to become rundown and neglected. The CCC-ID boys engaged in tree preservation, landscaping and erosion control, and weed and pest control. They fenced the entire school property, a huge job as the school had 160 acres of land, and they developed tennis courts and two outdoor picnic areas. With the help of a WPA crew, they also repaired and surfaced the campus roads. Because the CCC-ID boys were hardly older than some of the regular students, they were included in most campus activities. The only class exclusively theirs was one in First Aid, and that was taught by a Red Cross-certified instructor who was also a teacher at the Indian School. While the CCC-ID fellows were housed separately, they ate in the dining hall and socialized with other students at the school.

New Deal historians have often remarked on John Collier's skill in finding ways to circumvent the BIA's budgetary restrictions in pursuing his own goals. The CCC-ID enrollees at Phoenix Indian School provide an interesting example of his creative financing. The CCC-ID budget provided for the maintenance and continuing education of young Indian men who almost surely would have been thrown back on the strained resources of their tribes had they not been given work at the school. At the same time, their presence, financed by the CCC-ID, provided needed manpower for the maintenance of the school grounds at a time when the BIA's budget had become slender indeed. All the participants became winners in this situation, although Congress was not always pleased with Collier's budgetary manipulations.

Phoenix Indian School was forced to deal with several problems that resulted from the establishment of day schools on the reservations. One, already mentioned, was the need for staffing changes in the dormitories and in classroom instruction as the school's enrollment shifted. Another was the difficulty in supplying the new day schools with text books, library books, and other audio-visual materials. Phoenix Indian School provided a solution that had already been suggested at Carlisle Indian School in Pennsylvania. As the reservation boarding schools closed, their books were delivered to the Phoenix school, where they were catalogued by teachers from the various schools who donated some of their summer vacations to the task. Then they were loaded on a specially equipped library bus that delivered them to all the tribal day schools in southern Arizona. The bus eventually circulated about 15,000 books.[11]

Ideally the bus provided bi-weekly service to each of the twenty-three schools in the area, as well as to various CCC-ID camps. In addition to books, the bus carried phonograph records, magazines and stereoptical slides, and a generator so that it could show films for public viewing. The films were not always educational, of course. Comedies, westerns, sport films, films that were long on action and short on dialogue, were always popular, and short cartoons were also in demand. Schedules posted at each school with advance notice of the films to be shown generally guaranteed a good audience, although road conditions could cause that schedule to vary, of course. The Phoenix Indian School library bus provided an essential service to isolated Indian communities and permitted the day schools to provide many more books to their students and to isolated areas of the reservations than would have been possible otherwise.

Phoenix Indian School touched the lives of Indians in Arizona in still other ways during the 1930s. Some instructors became involved in federal extension services and provided two or three-week workshops in various Indian communities, aided by student interpreters. The workshops provided information on child care, household maintenance, and personal hygiene. They explained how to make such things as wooden furniture, using discarded shipping crates, and lye soap. A recipe for watermelon rind preserves proved extremely popular, especially since at certain times of the year there was no shortage of the basic ingredient.[12]

The school's community outreach also included a Diesel and Tractor School that began in 1933, when the Arizona Equipment and Tractor Co. of Phoenix invited some auto shop students to observe their maintenance operations. This first invitation developed into a short course at the school in diesel operations. In 1935, twelve men between the ages of eighteen and thirty-five were recruited from the reservations for four to six weeks of instruction in the maintenance and operation of heavy equipment. Classes were run by industry representatives, tuition was fifteen dollars, and room and board at the school were another fifteen dollars a month. As with the academic program, government loans were available for these very popular classes, and so were working scholarships so the men could live at the school and contribute to its maintenance.

Another very popular offering at Phoenix Indian School beginning in 1939 was a Telephone and Radio School, which originated as an aid to forest fire control. Classes were designed to prepare the students to meet the Federal Communications Commission requirements for a short-wave radio operators's license, and they included instruction in installation, maintenance, and operation of portable short-wave radio equipment. Graduates from these classes were immediately in demand, and they had no trouble finding employment with the Forest Service. Both the Diesel School and the Telephone and Radio School were eventually integrated into the National Defense Training Program.[13]

Most of the teachers at the Phoenix school were more than willing to try new programs, and they often led the way in further innovations. The school hosted the Arizona State Teachers Convention in November 1935, and at that time plans were developed for an Indian Service Section of the State Education Association. Two hundred Bureau of Indian Affairs educators attended that meeting, where Paul Fikinger, assistant to Indian Education Director Willard Beatty, spoke of changes in federal education policy for Indian schools. Out of this beginning came the Indian Bureau's first tentative experiments in bilingual education and in teaching English as a second language. Similar conferences were held at regional and local levels, and Phoenix Indian School representatives contributed significantly.

John Collier's various concerns left their mark on the Phoenix school in many ways. In addition to bilingual education, Collier was eager to develop markets for Indian arts and crafts, including those done by Indian students. Although in 1934 the federal Indian Arts and Crafts Board was still two years in the future, a new Indian Crafts Association in Phoenix established working arrangements with the Indian School to provide a market for student productions. Some of the boys and girls were talented artists, and the public was increasingly eager to buy their work. Under its agreement with the Crafts Association, the school kept half of the sales price of student art that was sold to the public. This fund was used to pay the association's dues and to buy art supplies. The students received the other half of the sale price. When members of the school's staff bought student art, they paid half the stated price, and the student received the entire amount.

Collier was interested in Indian art for two reasons. First, he considered it a valued expression of Indian culture with its own intrinsic worth. In addition, he realized that the sale of Indian art would bring significant economic benefits to the artists and their families. Dorothy Dunn's students at the Santa Fe Indian School in New Mexico were achieving a fair degree of public recognition, and Indian art was increasingly in demand. In 1936 the work of some students at Phoenix Indian School was even included in an exhibit at the Seventh World Conference of New Education in Cheltenham, England. Responding to increasing public interest, the BIA assigned Lloyd Henry New, a young Cherokee who had recently graduated from the Chicago Art Institute, to Phoenix Indian School as its art instructor.

New's arrival in Phoenix in 1938 brought him into contact with a number of young Indian artists, some of them students and some recent graduates who had remained on campus as teaching assistants. One was Andrew Tsihnahjinnie, known also as Van, a Navajo student who had studied under Dorothy Dunn in Santa Fe. Another was Hoke Denetsosie, also a promising young Navajo artist, who had graduated from Phoenix Indian School a couple of years earlier. A third was Charles Loloma, a Hopi student who was still two years away from graduation. When New arrived in 1938, Loloma was training for work in carpentry. Many years later he would be noted for his unique jewelry designs.

Loloma had already shown promise as an artist, and almost as soon as New arrived, the two young men left Phoenix together for San Francisco, where a commission was waiting. Under New's direction, Loloma and student artists from other Indian schools painted the murals that decorated the "Gallery of the Cornplanters," the Indian exhibit in the Interior Department's building at the Golden Gate Exposition. Loloma's portion of the mural depicted "an eagle, a buffalo, and a corn kachina descending on Hopiland early in the year." New and Loloma later went to Concha Indian School in Lawton, Oklahoma, to study advanced mural techniques under Olaf Nordmark, a Swedish master of mural painting.

When Loloma and New returned from Oklahoma, however, New faced a different assignment. He and Hoke Denetsosie, who were about the same age and later roomed together at the school, set out on a field trip through the Navajo Reservation, which until then was largely unknown to the new art instructor. This trip was part of a larger project taking shape at the Phoenix Indian School that had its origin in another of the Commissioner's concerns.

Collier had become increasingly frustrated over the difficulties the Bureau faced in trying to establish a stock reduction program on the Navajo Reservation. His people had come up against unexpected cultural impediments to a program that Collier and other soil conservationists considered essential if the grazing land on the reservation were to be restored after years of overgrazing. The difficulty resulted in large measure from an inability to communicate the necessity for stock reduction in terms that the Navajos could understand and would accept.

Viewing the problem in broad terms, Collier and Willard Beatty, Director of Indian Education, decided that part of the solution was to develop a technical Navajo vocabulary and invent a way to write the Navajo language so that the reasons for stock reduction could be explained more effectively. Earlier attempts had been made to develop a written Navajo language, but the results were designed for use by professional linguists, not for teaching Navajos how to read their own language. The phonetic symbols were far too complicated for children to learn, or for the convenient reproduction of printed material of any kind. Collier asked John Harrington, a linguist at the Smithsonian Institution, to develop a more practical system of writing Navajo.[14]

Another person soon to become involved in the project was Ann Nolan Clark, until recently a teacher in the day school at Tesuque Pueblo in New Mexico. Mrs. Clark had written a small booklet in English for her classes, and her students had illustrated it themselves. Her efforts were encouraged by Collier, who sent her to the Navajo country and then to the Phoenix Indian School to develop similar stories that might be translated and printed in Navajo. Hoke Denetsosie had been hired to do the illustrations, and his field trip to the reservation with Lloyd New was planned so that he could begin sketching for the new readers.[15]

Collier and Beatty assigned this project to Phoenix Indian School for two reasons. One, of course, was its proximity to the Navajo Reservation. The other was the fact that Phoenix Indian School, along with Haskell Institute in Kansas and Chilocco Agricultural School in Oklahoma, had printshops that were equipped with modern linotype machines. These three schools produced almost all of the printed material used by the Indian Bureau. The printshops were not at that time part of regular vocational training, as printing was a highly technical skill requiring many years of apprenticeship. Occasionally, however, a student with special interest would be assigned as the printer's assistant. Willetto Antonio, from the Navajo Reservation, was such a student at Phoenix.

From 1938 to 1942, artists Lloyd New, Hoke Denetsosie, and Andy Tsihnahjinnie, linguists John Harrington and his assistant, Robert W. Young, Phoenix Indian School printer Stewart Lewis, assisted by student typesetter Willetto Antonio, and Ann Nolan Clark cooperated in producing The Little Herder series of Navajo primers and several other books designed to teach Navajo children how to read their own language. Harrington and Young developed what is now considered standard, or "government," orthography. This new alphabet system was eventually imposed on an IBM typewriter ball for standard use. (As of 1990, IBM no longer manufactured the ball – a computer software program using government orthography had become the preferred device for writing the Navajo language.[16])

From 1938 on, the development of a standard orthography for the Navajo language, and then designing classroom teaching techniques, became major goals of the regular curriculum of BIA summer in-service workshops for teachers of Indian children in Arizona and New Mexico. At the first workshops, complicated questions of linguistics were discussed by Harrington, Young, and another BIA language specialist, Edward Kennard, while the young men from the Phoenix school, Hoke, Andy, and Willetto, provided essential assistance with the spoken Navajo. How to transcribe sounds onto paper, how to translate words for which there was no English equivalent, and how to develop a usable vocabulary, all had to be decided before the monumental task of compiling a standard dictionary could be completed. That task was finally accomplished, years later, by Robert Young. Edward Kennard and Charles Loloma later produced similar texts for Hopi children.

Translating from one language to another is never a matter merely of searching for word equivalents. Some words, phrases, or ideas are simply not translatable, and this problem led to the eventual failure of another Collier project at the school's printshop. Originally conceived as twenty-four posters illustrating simple ideas about health, safety, and agricultural practices, with illustrations to be done by Andy Tsihnah-jinnie, the poster project foundered on the difficulties of translation. Fairly obvious was one poster showing a farmer hoeing weeds in his field, originally captioned "Kill the weeds;" the messaage was translated more positively in Navajo as "Only the one who hoes has good corn." (See Appendix D) But white Americans were accustomed to sloganeering; in Navajo, the slogans often became ridiculous. "Put a red light on the back of your wagon" had the Navajos laughing at the idea of fastening a red light to the tail of their horses. Few of the posters were printed, and those failed to reach the wide distribution that was originally intended.[17]

The Little Herder Series eventually included four volumes, The Little Herder in Autumn, Winter, Spring, and Summer. The series was completed in 1942, with an initial run of the first volume of two thousand copies. Unfortunately, after Collier's resignation in 1945 they were little used, until the growth of tribally-run schools in the 1960s created a new demand for such material. New editions are now being printed by Treasure Chest Publications in Tucson, Arizona.

Hoke and Andy continued to draw and paint, and some of their work was included in an exhibit by the BIA's Education Division at the annual convention of the Progressive Education Society in Chicago in 1940. Andy later enjoyed moderate success as a painter, while Hoke illustrated a number of volumes for the Navajo Curriculum Center. Loloma painted other murals at the school and in buildings in the Phoenix area, but his artistic career soon moved in other directions.

Looking back at the decade prior to World War II, it is clear that those ten years had brought unforeseen changes to Phoenix Indian School. The school had met challenges within its own domain and had also explored new ways of serving the larger Indian populations in Arizona. While student life was not greatly affected by most of these changes, by 1941 there was an increasing awareness on campus of the need for national defense. Former students were enlisting in the armed services, and the CCC-ID men were beginning to realize that their skills might be needed some place far from their reservation homes. One organization, part of Phoenix Indian School since 1915, became increasingly important as the school moved into the next decade. That organization was Company F, 158th Infantry, of the Arizona National Guard.

2

Update - A Modern High School

In 1915, the United States had watched with apprehension the growing turmoil in Europe and, south of the Arizona border, the escalating revolution in Mexico. That same year, fifteen young men from Phoenix Indian School, all of them eighteen years old or older, enrolled in the Arizona National Guard as part of Company F, 158th Infantry Regiment, Fortieth Division. Ross Shaw, a Pima student at Phoenix Indian School, was one of those fifteen. Shaw would have graduated in 1916 had he not been with his unit, which was called up by the federal government for service against Pancho Villa on the Arizona border earlier that year.

Shaw and the rest of Company F were again activated in August 1917.[1] Although the unit went overseas that fall, the war ended in November, and the company saw no action. Two men from Phoenix Indian School, however, lost their lives in the war. Lee Rainbow, who was in the regular army, died in action, and Wallace Antone, who had been transferred from Company F to another unit, was killed just days before the fighting ended.[2] He was honored in memory when one of the boys' dormitories at the school was renamed for him. Company F had the privilege of serving as President Wilson's honor guard at the Paris peace talks, and Theodore Fierros, another member of the unit, recalled playing an exhibition game of baseball for England's King George V. The unit returned home for demobilization in 1919. The names of all who served were inscribed on a bronze plaque installed on the monument created by sculptor Emry Kopta, which was erected in front of Memorial Hall.

Company F took on new life when the Arizona National Guard was reorganized in 1924. From that time on, the all-Indian unit drew its members entirely from Phoenix Indian School and its alumni. As part of the 158th Infantry, the company was permitted to drill itself, to maintain its own armory at the school, and to conduct its own inspections. Like the band, Company F added to the public visibility of Phoenix Indian School, and it soon became a regular participant in various civic events.

During the 1920s and 30s, Company F consistently won awards, trophies, and championships for drilling, sharpshooting, and other aspects of military life. The school's military regimen had certainly taught the young men how to drill, and one of its members, Jasper Stewart, set a state record for the dismount and mount of the Guard's Browning Automatic Machine Rifle, for which he won a five dollar award.

On September 16, 1940, the Arizona National Guard was once again activated for federal service. During the next year, sixty-one men were called into active duty from Phoenix Indian School and from the Company F reserves under the command of four officers, Captain Stewart Lewis, an Indian School graduate who was also the school's printer, Captain Jacob F. Duran, a former school disciplinarian, and Lieutenants Truman Brown and R. P. Ballinger. Company F went first to Ft. Sill, Oklahoma, and then, reassigned to the 45th Division, it moved to Ft. Barkley, Texas, for further training. On December 8, 1941, the day after Pearl Harbor, the men headed for the Panama Canal Zone. While in Panama, the men of the 158th Regimental Combat Team, as it was now known, met the dreaded jungle snake, the Bushmaster, whose name they adopted as an appropriate symbol for their unit. Swelled by this time with men from every state in the union, the Bushmasters saw fierce action in the Pacific Theater, and they served with distinction in Australia, New Guinea, the Phillipines, and finally in Japan itself. [3]

National Guard members from Company F were not the only ones from the school who served in the armed forces during WWII. A number of former students also joined Company B, the National Guard unit from Mesa, Arizona, and they too served as part of the Bushmasters. Other former students served in all branches of the military, including the famed Navajo Code Talkers. During the war, letters came to the school from all over the world and were read to the assembled students. When deaths were reported, the flag on the Oval flew at half mast. Seven young men from Phoenix Indian School, two of them from Company F, lost their lives in WWII.

Phoenix Indian School was inevitably affected as preparations for war accelerated. Indian Commissioner John Collier offered all BIA facilities to the war effort – there was even some discussion at first of issuing arms to the Indians themselves in the event of an enemy invasion. Machinery, vehicles, hospital facilities, personnel, all BIA

resources were made available. For the most part, however, students
and staff did what people throughout the country were doing to help
America's war effort. They cancelled athletic trips to save gas and
rubber. They learned First Aid, and the school sponsored First Aid
classes for the community, as well. They saved rubber bands, paper, and
tinfoil, rolled bandages, bought war bonds and stamps, and donated
blood. A Civil Aeronautics Patrol, established in Phoenix in 1943, had a
unit of twenty-six boys at the school who served as official air raid
wardens.

Phoenix Indian School was also affected by the BIA's administration of the Japanese War Relocation Center at Poston, Arizona, on
the Colorado River Indian Reservation. Collier hoped to make that
center a showplace to illustrate his ideas of community self-government
as the Japanese-Americans settled there. But he also wanted to use the
internees' labor to develop a permanent irrigation system on some
20,000 acres of Indian land. Collier's plans for the future included using
that land for the relocation of Navajo and Hopi families whose
reservations were severely over-grazed, so he eagerly invested Indian
School resources of manpower and equipment in this effort. Construction equipment and agriculture personnel went to Poston, as did extra
school supplies, seeds, even some landscape plants. Although the BIA
retained control of the center only from April 1942 through December
1943, the irrigation system built at that time is still used by Indian families who farm there.

Another major project that reflected the school's war effort was the
development of a dehydration plant, which saved untold dollars by
preserving extra garden produce that would otherwise have been thrown
away. As food production on the school farms increased, the students
experimented with growing and dehydrating all kinds of fruits,
vegetables, and meat. [4] There was ample acreage at the school for a variety of crops, and while some varieties of produce did not dry effectively,
others kinds did. The school also traded for crops grown elsewhere, to
augment its own production. The staff showed its talent for
improvisation by building a series of three dehydrators, each larger than
the prior one, from odd pieces of equipment on the campus. Dehydration
was a relatively simple process, and the plant was operated chiefly by
students who received $2 a week for their labor.

An effort was also made to continue the national defense classes that had been started in diesel/tractor operation and telephone and radio use. By 1941, however, there were few enrollees, and eventually those classes closed for good.

Few traditions originated at Phoenix Indian School during the war years – like the rest of the country, the students and staff seemed to put "change" on hold until the war was over. There was one exception, however. A Nativity Pageant, produced for the first time in 1941, began a tradition for both the school and the City of Phoenix that lasted for over thirty years.

The school had traditionally celebrated Christmas, of course, and since most of the students stayed on campus during the holiday, the dining hall and dorms were always appropriately decorated. But the new pageant, written by one of the teachers and based on the Biblical Christmas story, was a full-scale production that at first involved not only students but faculty and staff, and even some students from nearby Cook Christian School. The school's various choral groups made up the choir, and they learned Hebrew chants along with traditional carols. They were accompanied, of course, by the band and orchestra.

The Nativity Pageant featured live animals in its manger scene, and the sheep themselves represented a school tradition that not many people knew about. Their connection with the school went back to the years following World War I. In 1919, the school decided to change the breed of sheep being raised on the school farm. The old flock was sold for eight dollars a head to Tommy McReynolds, Jr. Every year after that, Tommy McReynolds brought some of the descendents of those sheep back to the school for their role in the Christmas festivities, and the sheep continued to play their part in the new pageant.

The Nativity Pageant evolved over the years as an increasingly ambitious undertaking, and after 1945 it was totally a student production. Eventually several students shared each role, to allow as many girls and boys as possible to participate. In addition, students made almost all the sets and costumes. In 1943, Olaf Nordmark, the muralist from Concha Indian School in Oklahoma who had worked with Lloyd New and Charles Loloma in 1939, visited the Phoenix school and, among other things, helped paint new sets. In 1950, several teachers who had been to the Holy Land designed more authentic costumes, and in 1961, and again in 1971, the sets were rebuilt or repainted to keep them looking fresh and new.

The message of peace delivered by the angels at that first Nativity Pageant in 1941, just after Pearl Harbor, became a beacon of hope during the war for the school and the entire Phoenix community. From the beginning the students gave an extra performance for the people from town, and the school's Christmas pageant soon became part of the holiday tradition of the entire community. In 1952, for instance, over two thousand people from Phoenix attended two public performances. Members of the audience who were familiar with the various tribal languages represented by the students were always amused when they heard the familiar words of the Christmas story spoken with Navajo, Hopi, and Apache accents. It seemed that the Nativity pageant really did belong to all of them.

Although there was some talk once again of closing the school when the war ended, the Indians' wishes were clear. The military draft had made many people, Indians and non-Indians alike, realize just how many Indian children from various reservations still had not learned to read and write. In 1946 a group of Navajo ex-servicemen travelled to Washington to demand that treaty obligations dating from 1868 be met and that schools be provided for all Navajo children. The veterans' request surprised many people, because before the war the Navajos had been more interested in keeping their children out of school than in seeing them enrolled. But the veterans' war-time experience war had made them aware of their children's need to learn about the white man's world if they were going to survive in it.

This unexpected situation gave rise to an innovative program that soon brought new life to Phoenix Indian School. The school had emerged from the war with its basic mission still intact, to provide young Indians with the skills they needed to become independent members of the larger society. But while day schools were still teaching language skills and arithmetic on many reservations in southern Arizona, more than half of the schools established to the north on the Navajo reservation had fallen victim to economic starvation during the war and were closed. There were still several thousand Navajo children, now teenagers, who had never been to school, and many of them spoke no English. Responding to the demands of the veterans' delegation, the BIA decided that a crash course in basic skills must somehow be offered to all those young Navajos who had never been to school.

The Special Navajo Program (SNP) began at Sherman Institute in Riverside in the fall of 1946 and at Phoenix the following year. Eventually it was offered at ten of the BIA's off-reservation boarding schools. The largest number of students was enrolled at the Inter-mountain School in Brigham City, Utah, which at one time had over two thousand students. [5] Phoenix Indian School also taught hundreds of Navajo young people in the program.

Navajo youngsters who enlisted in the new program were between twelve and eighteen years of age, and none had had more than a year or two of school. They enrolled for five years, during which time, it was hoped, they would achieve the equivalent of an eighth grade education. For the first three years, they worked in ungraded classrooms, mastering language skills and basic math. The school acquired Sound-scriber recorders that allowed the pupils to hear themselves make the proper, or more frequently to their dismay, the improper, sounds as they struggled to master English pronunciation. Although language labs were commonly used at the time in many public schools to teach foreign languages, this was the first time such equipment was used to teach English to Indian children. Techniques for teaching English as a second language, developed experimentally by Robert Young and John Harrington in the years just before the war, were found to be effective and were further refined as the program got underway.

After the first three years of learning basic skills, students in the Special Navajo Program divided their time between academic classes and vocational training, which always began with learning the English names for tools and equipment. Girls enrolled in classes traditionally considered appropriate only for boys, and some of the girls became expert mechanics. At the same time, boys took home economics classes, so that when they lived in town they would know how to shop for food and prepare their own meals, how to launder their clothes, and how to maintain their living quarters. The BIA had started a program to relocate many young Indian families with job skills from reservations to cities, and the Special Navajo Program was designed specifically to prepare the students for this opportunity. At the Phoenix school alone, two hundred Navajo youngsters arrived the first year, and in each of the next ten years there were more, until by 1958 there were 427 Navajo students in the special program. In addition, almost 600 other students were enrolled in the regular program. By that time, new schools were once again being built in Navajo country, and the Special Navajo Program was phased out. No new students were accepted after 1958 – the last of the SNP students was graduated in 1963 – but by the time it ended, the program had served several thousand children altogether, and peak enrollment of all students at the Phoenix school had been over 1,100 students.

Although children in the Special Navajo Program attended their own classes for academic instruction and elected their own student officers in their living groups, they were encouraged to mingle with the regular students at all other times. They formed organizations and teams parallel to those of the regular students, and friendly rivalry between such groups added an element of excitement to campus life. The Navajo students took their turn in presenting assembly programs to the student body, and the Navajo choral group sang as part of the Nativity Pageant chorus each year. For ten years, graduation ceremonies included formal recognition of those who completed the five-year program.

Much of the success of the Special Navajo Program may be attributed to its innovative teaching techniques. In addition to the customary academic teachers, there were four teacher interpreters, young Navajos who were relatively fluent in both their own language and English. Many of them had been former students at Phoenix Indian School. These interpreters, together with the teachers, planned every lesson in advance, anticipating language and cultural difficulties. Then together they presented their lesson to the students and worked with them individually. The shop and home economics teachers or their aides were Navajo, too, so once again the students learned in both languages. The bilingual teaching teams proved highly successful.

Some of the Navajo students, of course, were not children by the time they finished, but mature young men and women. They had come to school highly motivated, and many of them made remarkable gains. Progressing at their own pace in the ungraded classes, some of them moved through three grade levels in a single year, and a number of them transferred into the regular school program and received their high school diplomas. Much of the credit for their success may be attributed to

Miss Beverly Queal, who directed the Phoenix program through most of its duration.

Phoenix Indian School was fortunate also during this entire period in having as one of its top administrators a seasoned veteran of Indian education, Glenn Lundeen, who came to the school as principal in 1947 to inaugurate the new program. Lundeen had previously served as an administrator in Indian schools at Fort Berthold, North Dakota, and Ft. Sill, Oklahoma. He and the Special Navajo Program started at Phoenix Indian School together, and they left at almost the same time – Lundeen moved to another assignment in 1965. By that time he had been superintendent for thirteen years, having been promoted from principal in 1952. He had watched the total number of students at the school mushroom, and it was his responsibility to house, feed and educate them all.

Not surprisingly, the advent of several hundred Navajo students at Phoenix Indian School produced an immediate crisis. With limited space available, the dormitories became terribly over-crowded. The school was still using Casa Saguaro and Wallace Antone, both built in the 1890s, as dormitories for older girls and boys. These old buildings were in various stages of decay – paint was peeling, stairs were dangerous, bathrooms were hopelessly inadequate, mice and cockroaches were commonplace, and fire was a fearsome possibility. When new students arrived, beds were put anywhere and everywhere. With school facilities stretched to the utmost, it became clear to everyone that the old buildings would have to be torn down and replaced as soon as possible. Meanwhile, attempts were made, with fresh paint and essential repairs, to keep the old buildings functional.

Although the buildings were clearly obsolete, they retained a sentimental value to many students at the time, who still recall with wistful smiles certain aspects of living there. A few of the older children always found ways to get up on the roof, where they could smoke cigarettes without being seen. Not only was smoking forbidden as a general rule, however; smoking on the roof was a double danger, as the old frame buildings were real firetraps. Casa Saguaro had spiral galvanized metal chutes for fire escapes (another forbidden place to play that some students found irresistible), and these would have been quite inadequate in case of a real fire. Scares were bad enough. An explosion in a fuse box one December night in 1948 made everyone realize more than ever just how dangerous the old buildings could be.

After that, the threat of a catastrophic fire was very real in the minds of Superintendent Charles E. Morelock and Principal Lundeen. Consulting the faculty at every step, they began to plan a long-range building program for new dormitories, class rooms, home economics facilities, and vocational shops. When Lundeen became superintendent in 1952, he asked for a BIA review, reevaluation and inventory of the entire school property. He also requested that the school be allowed to abandon Casa Saguaro – in fact, he had already begun to vacate the building. Some of the girls were moved from the second floor to the first, while others were relocated to the Employees Club, which for many years had been home to single members of the faculty and staff. The Employees Club was renamed Redwood Lodge at that time.

The BIA's report on the facilities at the Phoenix school led to the adoption of a building plan essentially as Lundeen and his staff had envisioned it. Over the next thirteen years, Congress authorized money for updating all the off-reservation schools, and the Phoenix campus was transformed into a modern educational complex. Included were eight new dormitories, an administration building, a materials center, five science classrooms with appropriate lab facilities, nine vocational and home economics units, and warehouse facilities. A modern gymnasium was added in 1974, although the earlier one, built in 1936, remained in use, as well.

The old dormitories were the first to be demolished. Casa Saguaro and Wallace Antone came down in 1953, and for a while the boys lived in army quonset huts until the first new dorms were opened in 1957. But that was only the beginning. One by one the other old buildings fell to the bulldozers. Even the steam whistle was a casualty. In 1953, the blast gave way to a "short toot," and by 1963, when a new power plant was built, it was gone entirely. The bandstand on the Oval, the site of so many important academic events, became another casualty at the same time, when the north end of the Oval was converted as the site of the new classrooms.

The new dormitories, the first buildings to be completed, had air conditioning and basement recreational facilities – TV rooms, vending machines, and pool tables. All were finished in March 1963, and they were dedicated with a grand celebration featuring Indian dances, a band concert, a fashion show, and a huge barbecue. Ground had been broken just the month before for the academic and administrative buildings, which became the new heart of the campus. A modern library, part of the materials center, was dedicated in September 1964 in memory of Gladys Nation, who had been librarian at the school for thirteen years. The new building complex faced north rather than south, toward the Memorial Hall and the dining hall, with a new flagpole and a fountain providing the central focus. [6]

Eventually only four old buildings, the dining hall, the Memorial Hall, the band building, and the old hospital, remained of the old campus. Each of those old buildings had a unique history. The dining hall, built in 1902, had originally been intended for use as an auditorium. Within a very few years, however, a kitchen was added, then a bakery and dish-washing facilities, and it had become the school's dining hall. The bakery soon developed an aura, or better an aroma, all its own. Many former students fondly remember Mr. Kilroy, who was almost as wide as he was high, presiding over the bakery in the 1930s and 1940s. He could be relied on to provide large, crusty loaves of bread which some of the students hollowed out and filled with other goodies from the kitchen, to be taken to the dorms for a midnight snack. (It was not that they were really hungry – there was always plenty of food at mealtimes. Their illicit snack was just one way of declaring their personal independence in a highly structured school environment, and Mr. Kilroy was their willing accomplice.) While the kitchen equipment was updated from time to time, the building itself remained basically unchanged. Fresh paint in 1975 led one student to comment that it was "new makeup for an old, old lady."

The band building, erected around 1930, was originally intended as an elementary classroom building. With the smaller number of younger students in the mid-1930s, however, it was taken over by the music department. The old hospital building, dating from about that same time, was converted into the recreation hall. Only the Memorial Hall, erected in 1922 in honor of those who died in WWI, remained as originally intended, a gathering place for the entire student body. With the Oval gone, the Memorial Hall became the old/new symbol of Phoenix Indian School. Once again the physical space of the campus was reoriented, with the change representing symbolically the fact that Phoenix Indian School had indeed become a modern high school.

The process of rebuilding the campus brought about one particular change in student life whose impact was gradual but profound in the long run. It began with the conversion of the old Employees Club building into a dormitory for the girls who had been living in Casa Saguaro. As a result of this shift, residents of the Employees Club, single faculty and staff members, had to find housing in town. Lundeen's family and others who lived on campus were obliged to do the same thing when their homes were torn down to make way for the new dormitories.

Until this time, faculty, staff, and students had all been part of a large school family. Although children of the faculty attended public schools in town, they often spent their free time playing with the students on campus, and many school meetings and other events were held in faculty homes. Teachers sometimes ate in the student cafeteria, and they met casually with students during the day as well as in the classroom. Not surprisingly, a family relationship developed with many of the children. But with the faculty living off campus and available only at scheduled hours on a more formal basis, those relationships began to change. Dorm matrons and aides became the primary contact with the students. While some teachers were pleased not to live on campus twenty-four hours a day, something vital had disappeared from the students' school experience.

Housing of the enlarged student body was just one of the many problems that beset the school administration in the 1950s. Feeding fifteen hundred faculty, staff, and students three times a day was another challenge. For one thing, the school increased the size of its dairy herd, which for years had produced enough milk for the entire student body. Students, agricultural faculty and aides, and a number of cooperative bulls helped keep the cows healthy and happy. Regular records were kept of each cow's milk production, and the entire operation, which was located on school property, was inspected regularly to make sure that quality standards remained high. Boys and girls on the two-week dairy detail got up at 2:30 AM for their turn at milking.

By 1952, however, the boundaries of the growing City of Phoenix had extended to the north and embraced the school property. Since livestock was prohibited within city limits, the dairy herd had to be sold at auction. A catalogue of all registered stock was prepared, along with the cows' production records, and sales were brisk. After the auction, milk for the school was purchased from a local dairy.

Although its dairy cows were now gone, the school continued to supply most of its meat by raising livestock in other places. It leased ninety acres of land east of Scottsdale from the Pima Indians on the Salt River Reservation and moved the hog farm from the campus to that site. It also leased 170 acres from the Colorado River Indians and raised a herd of 180 beef cattle there. The converted acreage at the school, enriched by generations of livestock manure, produced several crops of alfalfa a year, thus providing winter feed for the animals.

Students were involved in these various activities on a more sophisticated level than they had been earlier. They learned the latest livestock-raising techniques, how to operate complicated equipment, and how to keep accurate cost and production records. In other words, they learned the fundamentals of stock-raising as a commercial enterprise, not as an adjunct to subsistence farming. They also kept the school supplied with beef, pork, ham, and bacon. The students continued to grow fresh vegetables, but not on the scale produced during the war. The dehydration facility had long since been scrapped for additional classroom space.

Providing food and sleeping quarters for the regular students and the several hundred Navajo children demanded a good amount of improvisation, and so, too, did the problems of orienting new students to the school environment. Orientation was planned carefully and lasted over a period of several weeks. It actually began even before the children left the reservation, when some of the teachers visited the students in their homes. As part of the Special Navajo Program, teachers went to the reservation early and contacted returning students as well as those who would be enrolled in the new program. The school then contracted with Greyhound Bus Lines to send buses to various prearranged pick-up points. There teachers and returning students together welcomed the new children as they gathered for the bus trip to Phoenix. When they arrived at the school, the children were assigned to one of nine groups whose members became their classmates and dormitory companions. Considerable care was taken for the next several weeks to ensure their not feeling lost and abandoned. While English was encouraged, the old practice of punishing those who spoke their traditional languages had long since been abandoned.

Speakers at Phoenix Indian School graduation exercises in the 1950s struck a consistent theme, reflecting changes that had occurred in

Indian policy since the war. They told the graduates that, with proper education, they could find work anywhere in the booming post-war economy. They believed that education plus job skills would practically guarantee employment for anyone willing to work. But the young graduates faced a different reality. Even with marketable skills, many Indians still faced discrimination as they competed in the national job market. Government policy makers, however, refused to recognize this fact, and the Indian Bureau increased its efforts to relocate young families from the reservations into the cities where there were supposedly more job opportunities. Relocation had become part of a larger program of termination by which the federal government hoped to divest itself of responsibility for all Indian reservations.

This is not to say that the government succeeded in its efforts to relocate large numbers of reservation Indians or to terminate many tribes, only that these policies dictated various administrative and funding decisions made in Washington from 1947 to roughly 1965. The curriculum at Phoenix Indian School thus focused on providing skills that the students might use in the city rather than on the reservation. Girls were offered classes in typing, cosmetology, waitressing, retail sales, and practical nursing, while boys were encouraged to enroll in new academic classes in math and science.[7] Hildegard Thompson, who succeeded Willard Beatty as Director of Indian Education in 1952, was concerned about more young Indian people acquiring a college education, and she urged all the BIA boarding schools to upgrade their curriculum to prepare the students for college entry. When she visited Phoenix, she urged the students to work hard so that they could continue their education in academics or technical\vocational work. Under the new policies, their return to the reservation was not considered a viable option.

Although these curriculum changes met with some resistance from older teachers, most were willing if not eager to comply. For some, however, especially the vocational teachers, it meant going back to school for certification. Superintendent Lundeen and the school's principal, Thomas Tommaney, both enrolled at Arizona State College, where they earned MA degrees to comply with new Indian Bureau standards for school administrators. Reflecting these changes, Phoenix Indian School was accredited by the North Central Association of Colleges and Secondary Schools in 1960, thus indicating that it had met all requirements for teacher certification, was maintaining an adequate library, and had expanded curriculum and counselling services. With accreditation, the school's name changed – it became the Phoenix Indian High School.

The Bureau's renewed emphasis on relocation and termination, which was in many ways a modern garb for the pre-Collier policy of assimilation, was also reflected at the Phoenix school by the introduction of modern counselling techniques and a follow-up on the graduates after they left school. Job counselling became an important part of the Special Navajo Program. An expanded counselling staff took on job placement responsibilities and tried to maintain contact with former students who had relocated to see how they were coping. Lundeen, who agreed with Thompson on the need for an upgraded curriculum, was confident that their efforts in placing the Navajo students in urban jobs were successful. In 1953, he noted that "every one of the graduates last year, the first class to complete the five-year SNP, were placed. Few if any are back on the reservation. This, of course, is the payoff, and we are very pleased with the results so far." [8] Long-term follow-up of those relocated was never made, however, and later informal estimates indicated that the relocation program had met with only limited success. Many of those who relocated eventually moved back to the reservations.

Student activities at this time provided ample evidence of the impact of changing policies on Phoenix Indian High School. The annual Open House for students and their families, begun in 1949, proved so popular that some of the tribes chartered buses to bring entire families to the campus for the occasion. Acting as hosts, the students guided their relatives on campus tours, displayed their arts and crafts, presented a band concert, demonstrated traditional dances, and treated their families to dinner. What later became known as Indian Day continued the Open House tradition into the 1970s and 1980s, and in some years more than a thousand people attended.

The ever-popular dance group, no longer an adjunct of the Boy Scout troops, had become one of the most notable activities on campus, with a membership of as many as eighty boys and girls at any one time. The Phoenix Dons continued to provide major community support, and in 1955 some of the dancers performed on local television. In the summer of 1960, a small group of boys even went to Chicago, Cleveland, and

Cincinnati to dance as part of an advertising campaign for a new Phoenix resort, Superstition Ho.

The high point for the dance group during this period came in November 1957, when fourteen student dancers, accompanied by several teachers, travelled to New York City to perform at the Knickerbocker Ball, an annual affair held at the Waldorf Astoria. [9] The Knickerbocker Ball was a gala charity event, one of New York society's regular fund-raisers. Phoenix Indian School's participation was due in large part to Paul Coze, the same man who had produced the dance/drama "The Desert Way" at the school in 1939. Coze knew people in New York who were involved with the Knickerbocker Ball, and when its planning committee decided to feature the Indians of Arizona as its 1957 theme, it called on him. Proceeds were to go to a college scholarship fund for Native American students from the Southwest.

The Knickerbocker Ball was much more than just a dance. Guests first enjoyed an elaborate dinner, and on this occasion the menu featured foods of native American origin. These foods, however, would probably not have been recognized by most Native Americans. "Cream of Pumpkin Soup" was far more exotic than dried squash or pumpkin would have been, and "Turban of Maple Syrup," served as dessert, hardly resembled maple syrup as it came from the tree. The last item on the menu, "Tomahawk Coffee," left many people wondering about its origin.

The Indian theme reflected in the menu was carried over into the dining room decor. The tables and the room itself were impressively decorated with various Indian motifs crafted by students in the art classes at Phoenix Indian School. Life-size kachina figures were suspended from the ceiling, and table decorations and individual favors added to the Southwestern ambience.

Coze himself created another dramatic production, this time called "Lomatawi," Hopi for "The Good Song," which was presented to the guests after dinner. While its basic concept was quite similar to his earlier effort in Phoenix, "Lomatawi" was a much more elaborate affair. Once again, dances from four tribal traditions, this time Navajo, Hopi, Apache, and San Juan Pueblo, were featured as the story developed. While several of the dance groups were well-known professionals from the Southwest, the Navajo and Apache dancers came from Phoenix Indian School. Charles Loloma, who had long since graduated, designed the backdrop for the scene that featured a Hopi buffalo dance. According

to a press release issued by the Knickerbocker Ball's publicity committee, "many in the audience will be hearing and viewing, for the first time,
the true story of the Arizona Indian, including his cultural background,
philosophy, arts and crafts, and hopes for the future." [10]

While only a small number of people from Arizona actually attended
the New York event, the entire campus was very much aware of the
school's contribution to it. Many students had been involved in making
the decorations, and the dancers had performed several times, including
once on local television, before leaving for the East. The Knickerbocker
Ball provided national visibility, and the school's participation was pro-.
bably a factor in the invitation later received by the school band to march
in the Rose Bowl Parade of January 1959.

Although the band's role in the life of the school had diminished
somewhat after the military-style regimen was abolished in the 1930s,
and it had totally disappeared for a while in the 1940s, it was resurrected
after the war under the direction of Miss Rosemary Davey. Somehow she
managed to secure new instruments, and by 1950 another band, this
time with girls playing alongside the boys, brought new recognition to
the school. Its appearance in the Rose Bowl Parade marked the first time
any Indian school band had marched in that event, and the band was one
of only five high school bands from the entire country invited that year.
Unfortunately, while the parade was televised, many of the folks at home
were unable to see their boys and girls marching in it. The band was one
of the last units, and because the parade started late, NBC cut its
broadcast before they appeared to resume its regular programming.
When the band marched in the parade again in 1963, however, the whole
country saw it.

Something else also increased public awareness of Phoenix Indian
School at that time, and that was its athletic program. After the war,
boxing enjoyed renewed popularity when Elwood Hunter became the
Golden Gloves state welterweight champion, and he earned a trip to
Madison Square Garden for his efforts. Then for a number of years the
City of Phoenix cheered for the basketball teams coached by Joe
Famulatte, who came to the school in 1952. While Famulatte coached
football, baseball, and basketball, it was his basketball teams of the
1950s and '60s that repeatedly took state honors. One of the school's best
seasons was in 1957-58, when they won twelve games and lost five and
ended the season as Arizona State Class A Consolation Champions.

Basketball star Joel Querta scored a game record 53 points during the 1965-66 season, and the following year he was recognized by Sports Magazine as "Teenage Athlete of the Month." Ironically, that season's highlight was the school's loss to Globe, 121 to 112. That game set an all-time Arizona scoring record for high school basketball.

During the 1950s and '60s, Phoenix Indian High School was a consistent winner in a number of sports. Winning teams, encouraged by an enthusiastic group of cheerleaders, added many trophies to the school's trophy case. In fact, the athletic program was so successful that by 1964 the school boasted a new $30,000 playing field, complete with a scoreboard and cinder track.

Joe Famulatte, who coached at the Phoenix school from 1952 to 1975, was more than coach to the boys who played team sports. He and his wife loved them all and took more than one into their family at various times. Peterson Zah, who later became Navajo Tribal Chairman, was a member of that winning 1957-58 basketball team. After graduating, he attended Phoenix College and Arizona State, and during that time he made his home with his former coach. When Famulatte retired in 1975, part of the school's athletic spirit went with him, and when he was inducted into the Arizona Hall of Fame, Phoenix Indian High School proudly claimed him as their own.

Athletic competition remained an important part of school life, and the student newspaper, *The Redskin*, often devoted a large share of each issue to sports events. It wasn't just the winners who were mentioned, either. No item was too small. For instance, in 1953 *The Redskin* noted the appearance of new seventh grade baseball teams. The boys had come up with some really novel names for themselves. They knew about the Red Sox and the White Sox, so they decided to call themselves the Clean Sox and the Stinky Sox. The item was duly noted in the press.

The school's newspaper, called the *The Phoenix Redskin* since 1931, some time later dropped part of its name to become *The Redskin*. From its beginning as the *Native American* in the early years of the century, the paper had been a significant means of communication among the entire student body, and it contributed vitally to campus life. Written for the most part by the senior English class and later the journalism class, it was printed biweekly in the school's printshop. By the 1950s, its production was totally in the hands of students, providing them with an introduction to both journalism and printing as vocational options.

The newspaper staff was especially pleased to welcome Lloyd New and Ann Nolan Clark when they visited Phoenix in the 1950s and told the students of their experiences in producing "The Little Herder" series. Ann Clark remained at the school for a while to assist in the republication of *New Trails*, a book of student writings first published in 1931. Under her direction, the 1941 edition was enlarged with contributions from students in the Special Navajo Program, and it was republished in 1953. Unfortunately, by that time "The Little Herder" series was no longer being used to teach Navajo children to read their own language. [11] While English was taught as a second language in the Special Navajo Program, Navajo children were no longer taught to read their own language. That brief experiment, successful as it had been, had died with the war.

Nevertheless, by the 1950s, the school's printshop had attained a degree of fame for its involvement in printing the Navajo language, and the BIA invested in modern printing equipment for it. In addition to its Kelly C Automatic vertical printing press, the shop boasted of having a Bluestreak linotype machine, an ATF saw trimmer, a 36" power paper cutter, and a power stitcher. During this time, the school's capacity to print the Navajo language continued to further the cause of Navajo literacy on the reservation, if not at Phoenix Indian School. In 1942, Robert Young had begun to edit a monthly newspaper, which circulated throughout the reservation until 1957. First it carried news of the war and letters from Navajo service men, and then, after the war, information about government policies and other reservation news. Two thousand copies were printed each month, and enough Navajos learned to read the new printing to make it very successful. Young and Fred Snyder, who took over as printing instructor in 1947, also produced the first printed ballots to be used for an election on the Navajo Reservation. In addition, the Wycliffe Bible Translators published a number of readers illustrated by Andy Tsihnahjinnie, which were also printed at the Phoenix school.

Printing instructors Oliver Duffina and Fred Snyder taught the basic techniques of book binding as well as printing, which is why the paper cutter and the stitcher were acquired. Textbooks used in BIA schools throughout the country were shipped to Phoenix for rebinding. More students were also involved in the printshop operations, and those who chose printing as their vocational option had no trouble finding work after graduation. Unfortunately, a spectacular fire on May 24, 1962, destroyed the printshop and everything in it, with an estimated loss of $350,000, and its sophisticated equipment was never replaced.

One student who worked in the printshop and later enjoyed an enviable career, although not as a printer, was a young Mojave boy named Vincent Little. Vincent's twelve years at the Phoenix school reflect the opportunities that were available to all the students. He came to Phoenix in 1939 as a first-grader, one of the "orphan" children from an unstable family life, and stayed for twelve years to graduate. Vincent was a born leader. He was elected to a variety of student body offices, played in sports, and in the late 1940s, following Willetto Antonio's earlier lead, became an assistant to printer Fred Snyder. After graduating in 1951, he earned his bachelor's and master's degrees from Arizona State College, where he won the Gaylord Philanthropic Scholarship in 1956.

Vincent Little returned to Phoenix Indian School in September 1957 as junior class counsellor and teacher in the printshop. He also served briefly as superintendent of the school before his 1970 appointment as BIA area director in Portland, Oregon. He later retired from government service and established his own business in Albuquerque, New Mexico. Throughout his career he remained an important role model for students at the school.

Vincent Little was not the school's only student who grew into leadership roles after graduation. During the 1950s and 1960s, Ivan Sydney and Peterson Zah, who later served respectively as chairmen of the Hopi and Navajo tribes, and Leonard Haskie, interim chairman of the Navajo tribe in 1989-90, all attended Phoenix Indian School, went on to college, and developed independent professional careers before being called upon to serve as tribal officers. Many other tribal leaders in Arizona also received their education at the Phoenix school.

But there were other former students whose stories ended tragically. Best known, perhaps, was Ira Hayes, memorialized in the famous statue in Washington commemorating the flag-raising on Iwo Jima during World War II. After the war, Hayes had returned to Arizona, but he was unable to find a role for himself either in the tribe or in the outside world. He died in 1955, a victim of alcoholism. As one sympathetic reporter observed, "He was a hero to everyone but himself." [12] The students honored his memory, however, and when the statue was unveiled, the school band travelled to Washington for the occasion. The student body also established a fund in 1970 for an Ira Hayes Memorial, which was never built.

Many of the students at the school could identify more closely with Ira Hayes, perhaps, than with Vincent Little, for alcohol was a very present reality in their lives. Hardly a family escaped the trauma caused by excessive drinking, and some of the students themselves came to school with alcoholism already a personal problem. From the school's earliest years, the grim toll taken by alcohol had provided a tragic counter-point to student life. After the war, as transportation became more available, visiting parents sometimes arrived drunk, and sometimes students returning to the campus were drunk. No one really had an answer to the problem, but students with disruptive behavior were generally expelled. While expulsion failed to help the offender, it may have kept the disease from spreading at the time. Alcohol abuse at the school would later become epidemic.

A story that might be amusing had it not had such serious overtones concerned a fire that destroyed a commercial establishment across the street from the school in the 1950s. The store sold packaged liquor, among other things, and as the liquor bottles heated in the fire they exploded. Students who came out to help fight the blaze "rescued" all the bottles they could find and cached them away in various places on campus. School authorities found some of them, but evidence of the "rescue" operations was all too apparent among the students for some time after the fire.

During the 1950s and 1960s there was increasing evidence that Phoenix Indian High School was losing its vocational focus and becoming more and more like other American high schools. Not only had it achieved accreditation, in 1956 it was also finally admitted to the Arizona Interscholastic Association, which allowed it to compete in team sports with public high schools in the area. It became involved with other city-wide student activities, as well. Its long-time association with the YMCA and YWCA and their Y-Teen groups led to the first Arizona meeting of "Anytown U.S.A." at the school in 1952. "Anytown U.S.A." appealed to teen-agers with a message designed to break down barriers between ethnic groups by stressing a common American identity. A group of California teens sponsored by "Anytown U.S.A." stayed on campus during the weekend event, and later forty-five Phoenix students paid a reciprocal visit to their guests' families in California. One student was the guest of a black family, an unforgettable experience for her. The students wrote enthusiastic essays about their hosts, portions of which were printed in *The Redskin.*

Students also began to establish more normal, one-to-one relations with members of the Phoenix community during this period. The outing system noted earlier, with its voluntary participation in a Saturday work program, remained popular with the students. Demand was especially strong for girls who did housework, and often there were more requests than there were girls to fill them. Such work provided the students with an opportunity to earn some money, and it also gave them a chance to get away from the campus and develop a more realistic sense of urban living.

The school also encouraged local businesses to hire students, and this generally worked to the satisfaction of all concerned, although occasional conflicts did occur. Boys seemed to find adjustment to outside jobs more difficult than girls did, perhaps because they were less amenable to taking orders. Wages for student help remained low, and the boys may also have been more sensitive to the possibility of being exploited.

Students who worked on Saturday generally got paid at the end of the day, and this created an urgent problem: where to keep their money over the weekend. The problem was solved by the establishment of a student bank on campus that stayed open late on Saturday. The idea soon evolved from an informal arrangement at the school to regular savings accounts with Valley Bank. The bank sent representatives to explain how banking systems worked and how as depositors the students retained control of their money, even though they had put it in the bank. The school encouraged each girl and boy to save seventy-five dollars for graduation, to pay for year books, cap and gown rentals, photographs, and other incidentals. Some students saved enough money to buy their own clothes and tickets home for Christmas.

Responding to the new availability of spending money, students, with faculty help, also established a store that first opened in the basement of Memorial Hall. Here they could buy candy bars and gum, stationery supplies, toiletries, and other incidentals. Student clerks behind the counter learned how to make change, maintain an inventory, and keep the customers happy. The store was very successful, and eventually it moved into more spacious quarters in one of several small buildings on campus that the construction trades classes had built for various purposes.

A number of Saturday jobs came about through contacts made by the students at the churches they attended. Superintendent Lundeen believed that the churches provided a stabilizing effect on student life, and he encouraged their presence on the campus. Cook Christian Training School continued to provide religious education until 1956, when Dr. Logie retired. Lundeen then obtained funds from the National Council of Churches to hire Dr. Harold Lundgren, an ordained Baptist minister, to serve the school community. Dr. Logie and Dr. Lundgren were assisted on occasion by the Rev. Roe B. Lewis, a Pima from Gila River Reservation. Dr. Lewis was a Presbyterian minister who had earned his B.A. degree from Arizona State Teachers College in Tempe. He had done his practice teaching at Phoenix Indian School in 1940 and was also on the teaching staff for a brief period. Roe Lewis's ministry to the entire Phoenix Indian community became well known, and a number of former students returned to Phoenix so that he could officiate at their weddings. For some students, the religious training offered at the school was vitally important. For others, however, it had little if any significance.

The year 1965 began another period of transition for Phoenix Indian High School and for Indian education nationally. Glenn Lundeen had become superintendent in 1952, the same year that Hildegard Thompson was named Director of Indian Education for the BIA. Thompson resigned in 1965, and Lundeen transferred to a new position with the Indian Bureau in Washington, D.C. at the same time. The two educators had shared a common philosophy concerning the role of the off-reservation boarding school – it was to offer Indian children the opportunity to learn adaptive skills so they could live satisfying lives in the larger society. Like their predecessors, they believed that assimilation was inevitable in the long run, and that even if Indian people chose to retain their cultural identity, some degree of adaptation was essential for their survival. Off-reservation boarding schools, especially one like Phoenix that was in such close proximity to a large urban center, could continue to play a significant role in that adaptation. But even as the Phoenix Indian High School dedicated its new buildings in 1965, there was talk once again of closing it or changing its essential role in Indian education. Its future remained uncertain.

3

The Mandate Outgrown

S tudents attending Phoenix Indian School in the mid-1960s were unaware of any dramatic changes during their high school years. James D. Wallace, who replaced Glenn Lundeen as Superintendent, had been principal there since 1955, and the transition to the new administration went smoothly. Teachers commented favorably on the well-disciplined students, and they enjoyed the new classrooms and library. Students appreciated the relative luxury of the new dormitories. Although there had been muted talk once again of closing the school or converting it into another kind of facility, student life appeared much as it had been in the past.

Shifts in the curriculum from year to year, however, were reflecting changes in Indian education policy at the national level.[1] Hildegard Thompson had been a strong advocate of post-high school training in both academic and vocational/technical areas. She had pushed for the development of a college preparatory curriculum at the boarding schools, including courses in algebra and advanced mathematics, the physical sciences, and architectural drafting. In carrying out these policies, Lundeen had encouraged students with academic potential to remain at the school on a working scholarship during the summer so that they could attend summer-school classes at nearby Central High and make up academic deficiencies for college entrance. Some students took advantage of these advanced classes and continued their education after graduation. Many did so well, in fact, that Phoenix Indian High School sponsored a chapter of the National Honor Society. It was the only BIA school in the country to have such a chapter.

As the academic offerings were strengthened, however, the vocational program suffered. Intensive shop classes were limited to the junior and senior years, so the students had less time to develop skills that would be of immediate value in the labor market. To supplement their training, they were encouraged to continue their studies at Phoenix City College or Haskell Institute in Oklahoma, which was establishing new post-graduate programs in electronics, the building trades, and various service occupations, in addition to its business courses. From the class of 1958, for example, nine graduates went on to college, while twenty others entered advanced vocational training.

This was only about twenty percent of the total senior class, however. Most of the graduates were not interested in continuing their education. A 1966 Reevaluation Report described Phoenix Indian School students overall as being three or more years behind grade level for their age, and many still had severe language problems.[2] In response to this report, nearby Arizona State University offered to juniors and seniors an all-Indian Upward Bound program which, like the summer sessions at Central High, was aimed at correcting deficiencies in math, English, and social studies. In the summer of 1968, Upward Bound drew forty students for the four-week session. But the majority of graduates, not interested in going to college, were increasingly ill-equipped for the real world that lay ahead of them.

Thompson had responded to a variety of pressures in pushing the academic program in Indian schools. Russia's launch of Sputnik and the subsequent review of U.S. education had sent shock waves through the entire educational establishment and increased the demand for more rigorous classroom instruction in all schools, including those run by the BIA. Those who advocated termination of the tribal relationship also favored an enriched academic program because they believed that it augmented the assimilation process. So Thompson disregarded the fact that a great many Indian people wanted the school to continue its traditional emphasis on vocational training. Even if she had so desired, she would have found it extremely difficult to maintain the old industrial training programs in view of the existing climate of educational reform, relocation, and termination in the 1950s and '60s.

The new emphasis on academics at the Phoenix school was reflected not only in the classroom but also in a variety of campus activities with a decidedly urban, main-stream orientation. Students organized a Free Enterprise Club, to learn how small businesses operate. They sponsored a number of fund-raising activities and gained valuable experience in advertising, investments, and profit-sharing. Members of a club called Med-Start were interested in careers in medicine, and a Leadership Club established in 1969 attempted to develop Indian leadership through the practice of group dynamics. They invited role models from the community to share their experience as leaders in a variety of situations and enterprises.

In the 1970s, the students also expanded the boundaries of their world by inviting out-of-state and foreign students to the campus. Two young non-Indians from Massachusetts and Indiana enrolled for a year in 1973, and later there were students from Ireland, Yugoslavia, Ghana, and Finland. At meetings of the United Nations Club, interested students learned about those and other places and about the intricacies of world politics and economics. As a result of their overseas contacts, ten members of the Apache Club, which was noted for its performance of the traditional Mountain Spirit Dance, spent part of their 1979 Christmas holiday in Ireland.

There were other kinds of outreach, as well. During the Christmas holidays of 1968, girls from the cosmetology class paid a visit to the Indian Hospital, a mile or so from the campus, not to sing carols but to give patients morale-boosting gifts of shampoos, hair stylings, and manicures. During the dedication of the new Phoenix Indian Hospital in 1970, girls in traditional tribal dress served as hostesses and guides.

Some of the traditional student clubs also maintained good membership. Although Boy Scout Troop 27 had been disbanded, members of Troop 5 became Explorer Scouts and remained active until 1986. The various dance clubs, often organized now by tribe, continued to attract both boys and girls during the 1970s. Dancing became more popular than ever as renewed interest in Indian identity reflected growing ethnic awareness, and various tribal clubs flourished.

The school also felt the effects of the war in Vietnam in the 1970s. While Company F, the National Guard unit, had not been reorganized on campus after World War II, there was a resurgent interest in military affairs. In 1968, the Marine Corps Junior Reserve Officers Training Corps (MCJROTC) established a platoon at the school, and Colonel Clay A. Boyd, Commander of Company F, attended its opening ceremonies as guest of honor. The Marine Corps Junior ROTC boasted 160 members, including a girls' auxiliary unit. Under student leader Captain Barney Fielding, members spent ninety-six hours a year drilling and studying military science and combat techniques. Cadet Larry Noline, who earned the rank of Master Gunnery Sergeant, visited Washington one year as a representative of the Marine Corps Youth Program, and the entire group spent a week at Camp Pendleton in California in April 1970. The Corps remained part of school activities until 1975.

The presence of the military unit at the school led to an unusual opportunity for students to participate in a world-class sporting event. The National Rifle Association (NRA) held its 40th World Shooting Championships at the Phoenix Trap and Skeet Club in 1970, and more than four hundred students from the school provided logistical support. Each of the boys and girls worked for thirteen days. They operated telephones, loaded and pulled targets, and did whatever else was needed. Their pay of $1.75 an hour was only part of their reward. They wore a cowboy hat, kerchief, jeans, cowboy shirt, and a belt with a commemorative buckle, all of which were provided by the NRA and became theirs to keep when the event was over. They also had an opportunity during their work to meet representatives from sixty-two different countries.

The most ambitious excursion taken by a large number of students from Phoenix Indian High School occurred in July 1983. Sixty band members, along with that year's Miss PIHS, Claudell Jones, and three of her attendants, and band director Miss Ileane McElwee, flew to Philadelphia and Washington, D.C. In the nation's capital they marched directly behind President Reagan in the city's annual Fourth of July parade. Wearing feathered headbands and either ribbon shirts or Navajo-style velveteen shirts, white or blue trousers, concho belts, and moccasins, they were real crowd-pleasers in several other appearances during the trip. Band members themselves had raised $50,000 to pay for their expenses. Throughout its history, the band had provided the greatest public visibility for Phoenix Indian School, both in the local community and throughout the country.

Athletic activities, as usual, held student interest until the school's closing – even during its last year, 1989-90, Phoenix Indian High School had a competitive basketball team. With decreasing enrollment in the 1980s, however, varsity football fell on hard times. Although the school had been admitted to the Interscholastic Association in 1957 and had played a regular conference schedule, its students were unable to compete with other teams in size. After years of showing poorly against the stronger teams, the school asked for the association's permission to play independent schools once again. In 1978 it played Sherman for the first time since 1940, and won. The Phoenix school defeated its old rival quite consistently over the next several years. It was also more competitively matched against other Indian schools. In 1980 the varsity team, which usually travelled by bus, enjoyed a trip to Brigham City, Utah, by plane for a game with Intermountain Indian School.

During the 1970s, Phoenix Indian High School also fielded a winning girls basketball team led by Rita Ventura, who set a state record by averaging 26.2 points per game. The newspapers called her "a 5'2" scoring machine." Crowned Miss Papago, Rita excelled in academics as well as sports. As an honor student, she won a three thousand dollar tribal scholarship to Ft. Lewis College in Durango, Colorado. While the boys at Phoenix Indian High School had more opportunities to shine in athletics than the girls did, Rita Ventura demonstrated the girls' potential with her all-around superior performance.

While Phoenix Indian High School sponsored many of the activities typical of other modern high schools, and shared some of their concerns, as well, its problems sometimes revealed its unique origins. Discussions over the proper length of hair worn by male students, common to high school students everywhere, turned into arguments with such an impact that the "hair controversy" made its way into the student newspaper and the year book. The question at the Phoenix school developed ethnic overtones, since not too many years earlier, Indian boys had been forced to cut their hair when they went to boarding school. In 1973, Anselm Antone, nicknamed "Hair," was elected vice president of the senior class, and his photograph in the year book, with long hair, suggests the popularity of his cause. A comparison of the 1973 year book with that of 1968 reveals a widespread adoption of long hair styles by both boys and girls, as a display of ethnic identity.

Renewed student interest in their Indian identity, reflected to some extent in the hair controversy, was sparked by Lee (Lehman) Brightman, director of the Indian Studies Program at the University of California at Berkeley, who visited the campus in March 1970 and again in October 1972. His long braids, when he came the second time, reflected the new Indian awareness. After he spoke of "red power," which had become a rallying cry for Native Americans in the late 1960s, the formerly quiet and well-disciplined students began to demand their "rights," to cut classes, and to challenge the school's authority in ways that would have been unthinkable just a short time before. Student protest spilled over into the dining hall when students working on cafeteria detail were verbally attacked by other students waiting to be served. This abuse continued until Miles Bollinger, principal from 1969 to 1980, secured peace by hiring outside help for the cafeteria and promising that the following year students themselves would receive pay for cafeteria work. Students were very much aware of escalating campus unrest; in the 1973 year book, one caption proclaimed that "the Student Council remains active in spite of troubles."

Other disruptive elements from the outside were also beginning to impinge on the school in ways that soon became quite obvious. Congressional measures that had financed the new buildings on the Phoenix campus had also provided funding for new high schools on many of the reservations, once again causing shifts in the school population. Paved roads, better school buses, and federal subsidies for Indian children attending public schools were making both public high schools and reservation schools accessible to more students than ever before. Many Indian children now had the opportunity to attend high school near home rather than in off-reservation boarding schools. As a result, an ever-growing portion of the Phoenix school's student body consisted of young people with family or social problems or learning disabilities, who were sent to Phoenix because they were unable to adapt to the local schools. By the time they reached Phoenix Indian High School, their problems were often so deeply entrenched that they disrupted the educational program, and the school lacked the resources to deal effectively with them. [3]

As unruly students threatened to disrupt traditional activities, school administrators were faced with new questions about the nature and purpose of discipline and ultimately of the entire off-reservation boarding school system. From the earliest days, the boarding schools had been entrusted with the job of instilling in Indian children the middle-class values and work ethic common to American society at the time. But now the larger society itself was increasingly concerned with what it perceived to be "a loss of traditional values" among all of America's young people. Some educators were arguing that the old values, which were culturally derived, were relative only to the society in which they had originated, and that society had changed. The old values were said to be stifling. They inhibited creativity, contributed to feelings of guilt, were culture-ridden, and obstructed the free flowering of cultural pluralism. Children were encouraged to "find their own way," to "do their own thing," in a society that was questioning its own definition of right and wrong. Teachers were no longer sure that old-fashioned discipline was necessary or even desirable. Many Indian children, especially those whose tribal value systems were supposedly being replaced by those older traditional "American" values, were set adrift.

Glenn Lundeen had not been plagued by such doubts and uncertainties. He believed that discipline, in the form of rules that were both necessary and enforceable, was essential if the school was to run smoothly. Children from the reservations needed to be taught not that the ways of living at home were wrong but that they were different. The urban environment demanded new kinds of behavior, and to act otherwise was not necessarily bad but inappropriate and would provoke an unpleasant reaction from the outside world. Lundeen entrusted the students with considerable freedom, along with campus discipline, because he believed that those values were being taught and internalized, and that the students would behave in an acceptable fashion. For the most part, he was not disappointed.

There were few policy guidelines, however, for Lundeen's successors. Indian educational policy was itself undergoing change at a time when the school was admitting more and more students with serious behavioral problems. By "letting them find their own way," the school administration was forced to rebuild the school fence, to limit the students' freedom, and in extreme circumstances to impose physical restraints.

In the face of growing problems, the question inevitably arose, then, concerning the role of the school: was its primary concern to be with education or with behavior modification? No one was prepared to answer that. Meanwhile, troubled young people were steadily becoming a larger percentage of the student population, and their behavior caused serious interruptions in the classrooms. When the public, Indian and non-Indian alike, became aware of the disruptions, they increasingly questioned the value of the school.

It was symptomatic of the values question that some old traditions fell during the 1970s, as traditions do when they no longer seem relevant. One of the casualties was the annual Nativity Pageant. An anticipated event in Phoenix since the early 1940s, its last regular production was in 1972. Some students attempted to revive it in 1978, "the first time in many years," according to the student newspaper, but that 1978 performance was the last one. The demise of the Nativity Pageant became a metaphor for failed Indian education policy. Every year the school had printed a souvenir program for the pageant, decorated with traditional Christmas motifs. Only once, during the years of the Special Navajo Program, did the program, or the pageant itself, for that matter, depict the Christmas story as pertinent to Indian life. That one program showed a Navajo shepherd gazing at the Christmas star. But the Christmas story, encrusted as it was with all the trappings of western European culture, seemed increasingly irrelevant to Indian life, and the students had lost interest in it.

Christmas continued to be a school holiday, of course, but other pageantry and other celebrations now competed for the students' interest. The first Miss PIHS contest was held, perhaps not coincidentally, in 1973, and "Indian Day" replaced "Open House" as the traditional visiting day for the students' families, although the activities were much the same as they had been since 1949.

The election of Miss PIHS illustrated still another element of cultural disparity. Student elections had become nothing more than popularity contests. It was fun to win the election, and winning became the goal. While candidates vied for class and student body offices, few of the winners served out their terms. They found little satisfaction in following through with the responsibilities of the office they had won.

In fact, if the student newspaper accurately reflected campus morale, students were finding little satisfaction in anything they did. The few organized free-time activities on campus had little student support. "Ho-hum" was a standard response to the daily routine. Nothing was a challenge any more. Vocational interests lagged, cheerleaders chatted among themselves and failed to arouse school spirit, club memberships dropped, and a general malaise began to set in.

The one exception to this growing antipathy was the renewed interest in Indian culture and identity, as evident in the students' long hair and the growing membership in tribal clubs. And the young people's open rejection of certain aspects of white culture that seemed increasingly irrelevant to Indian life was a national, not just a local, happening. The most cogent summary of critics' views at the time was published in 1972 by Robert J. Havighurst and Estelle Fuchs. Their book, titled *To Live on This Earth*, provided a synthesis of the U.S. Office of Education's 1970 critique, *The National Study of American Indian Education: The Education of Indian Children and Youth*. [4] Those engaged in the study had been dismayed to discover that Indian education generally was almost as ineffective as it had been in the 1920s. But their report also revealed a new understanding of the need for direct Indian participation in the education of their children. A renewed demand for bilingual education, for text books written in native languages, and for materials focused on tribal culture and history, suggested that crucial changes were again taking place.

After generations of trying to convert Indian children to fit an "American" model, critics were finally beginning to recognize that Indian education must be determined by the Indians' need to live in two cultures, not one. Some critics were also finally willing to admit that no one knew better than the Indians themselves how their educational goals should be defined. No matter how well-meaning the educational establishment, Indians themselves must demand, and accept responsibility for, control of their children's education. Public Law 93-638, the Indian Self-Determination and Education Act, passed in 1975, was a giant step in this direction. [5] It was now up to the Indians themselves to redesign Indian education. Hesitantly at first, independent school districts organized in response to that law, patterned after those at Zuni Pueblo and at Ramah and Rough Rock on the Navajo Reservation. For the first time, Indian people elected their own school boards and decided matters of curriculum and personnel.

These moves toward self-determination were more effectively applicable to local schools, however, than they were to the Bureau's off-reservation boarding schools. Although an inter-tribal school board was established for the Phoenix Indian High School, getting the board members together for meetings was extremely difficult, and decisions continued to be made by the Indian Bureau Area Director and his education program staff. At one momentous time, however, the School Board of the Phoenix Indian High School did exercise its power to the fullest. In 1986 it obtained the removal of Principal Richard Christman, citing the lack of discipline among the students and a failure to communicate with the parents. What led to those charges was a long, sad story.

Dr. Frank Clarke, who worked part time as a counsellor for troubled and addicted students at the school, had presented some frightening statistics in a January 1986 article in the *Arizona Republic* written by Linda Helser. [6] According to Dr. Clarke, 256 students, out of a total of 700, were expelled during the 1984-85 school year for vandalism,

substance abuse, violence, cutting classes, and related anti-social behavior. One fourth of the remainder were also considered abusers, primarily
of alcohol. The school board, backed by the Inter Tribal Council, accused
the principal of hiding the extent of the problem for fear of negative
public reaction. The students themselves had called attention to the
situation by forming a support group, "Indian Students Against Drug
Dependency," to combat the rising tide of substance abuse on the
campus.

Dr. Clarke was not the first, however, to call attention to worsening
conditions at Phoenix Indian School. Two previous articles published by
New Times, a Phoenix area weekly, had been extremely critical. In
January 1980, *New Times* reporter Tom Kuhn had written an expose
entitled "Phoenix Indian School: The End of the Rope", in which he
focused on the school's increasingly severe problem with alcohol.[7]
Occasional drinkers, he said, were becoming drunks at the school, and
tribal turf battles and sex parties were spilling over from the campus into
nearby neighborhoods. He claimed that the students were ill-served by
being "segregated" in what he called a "military post." Offenders should
be brought before the city's courts, he insisted, not insulated from public
reaction behind the walls of the school.

Students reacted to Kuhn's article with outrage in *The Redskin*.
They charged that it was a one-sided, biased report based on interviews
with only four students, who were then quoted out of context. Kuhn had
looked only for the bad side of student life, not the good. But when the
students had cooled off a bit, they admitted that there was truth in what
Kuhn had said. Alcohol was a dark part of the reality of school life for
both boys and girls, and normal discipline was increasingly ineffective.

Some remedial measures had been taken at the school, although the
rationale for them was not always clear. One was the elimination of the
merit system that had been in place since the 1930s. Instead of merits,
good behavior was to be rewarded with an opportunity to live in the
Honor Dorm, thus reinstituting a policy of some years earlier.
Montezuma Hall, another dormitory, was converted into a kind of half-
way house that supposedly provided a more supportive environment for
those in danger of expulsion and for those already expelled who had been
accepted conditionally for readmission. Boys who were assigned to
Montezuma Hall lived there for at least four weeks, but as rehabilitation
the arrangement was not very effective. The troubled ones received

inadequate counselling, and disciplinary problems among them became pervasive and overwhelming.

The counselling staff at the school was poorly trained, under-staffed, and under-funded during this critical period when it was being asked to assume responsibility for treating children with severe emotional and learning disabilities. The new supervisor of the counselling department knew very little about American Indians – she had lived in Japan and France, and had for the prior twelve years been a counsellor in a high school in Palos Verdes, California, a wealthy seashore community south of Los Angeles. [8]

The teaching staff was also weakened during this period by a Congressional reduction-in-force law passed in December 1979. Nicknamed the "Honkey Bill" or the "Early Out Bill," it allowed for early retirement of senior personnel and invoked Indian preference for positions thus vacated. At the Phoenix school, twelve staff people, including the principal and the assistant principal, retired the following spring. [9] The six with the longest service records represented one hundred years of experience at Phoenix Indian School. While some of the twelve were scheduled to retire in any event, together they represented a body of experience not easily replaced. Some of their positions remained unfilled, primarily because of shrinking budgets, and this resulted in a critical shortage of experienced, qualified teachers.

Surely there was enough blame to go around. It is possible to look back and see how the situation worsened, but it was harder to discern the pattern at the time. The demolition of the old buildings that resulted in the teachers and administrators moving away from the campus and from intimate contact with students might be seen in retrospect as the beginning. Add to that the changing nature of the student body, the reduced emphasis on vocational training, the frustrations of poorly prepared students from reservation day schools trying to cope with the new academic curriculum, the rise of a new sense of Indian identity and empowerment among the students – all these factors had interacted to produce the growing conflicts at Phoenix Indian High School.

Conditions continued to worsen until, in early 1981, a suit was filed against the school in U.S. District Court in Phoenix by two former students. Although both had a long record of previous infractions, they claimed that they had been denied a hearing when they were expelled from the school by principal John Derby. Their case eventually became a class-action suit and was pending until 1988, when it was finally settled out of court. The suit was significant, however, because evidence produced by the plaintiffs included pages from the school's security log that revealed the extreme measures being used by the school to control its students. The log spoke for itself, and school and area authorities made no attempt to disprove its contents, only to justify the actions described in it.

While the suit was moving through the court system, Richard Christman, a veteran of twenty-two years with the Indian Bureau, was appointed principal. When he arrived at Phoenix, Christman found the situation acute, and he was unable to change the direction in which the school was moving. "I feel these are longstanding conditions," he said in response to criticism of the school's disciplinary methods. "In fact, some of the reasons our students are sent to Phoenix is because of high absenteeism, dropping out and discipline problems. . . . If I discipline them and send them home, they may have lost their last chance. Besides, as soon as I discipline a student, we have attorneys calling us." [10]

In late 1984, *New Times* published a second article, this one entitled "Handcuffs and Too Little Hope: Atypical Education at the Phoenix Indian School," by reporter Andy Zipser. [11] By this time alcohol was not the only problem at the school. Zipser claimed that marijuana and other substances were openly used on the campus, and that the only controls seemed to be extreme forms of physical restraint. The counselling staff, he claimed, was totally unable to deal with the escalating problems. Zipser then presented data from the Arizona Department of Education and the Phoenix Indian Center to show how badly the students at a number of Indian high schools in the state, not just at Phoenix, were performing academically. Why, he wanted to know, were Indian parents, tribal councils, and the Indian school boards not demanding that something be done.

The answer to that question was not simple. Most pervasive and difficult to overcome was Indian inertia, which had evolved through decades of reaction to the paternalistic authority of the BIA. Tribal leaders and members of the School Board, all of whom were miles away from Phoenix, had not been informed of the situation, nor had they seen the evidence presented in the law suit. When they asked for information, they were told by school and Indian Bureau officials that they were working on the problem, and there was no need for the board to worry about it.

In addition, many parents, as well as members of the various tribal councils and the School Board, had themselves been students at Phoenix Indian School, and their selective memories refused to admit that such things could be happening there. At the same time, however, there was tacit acknowledgement that many students had had problems before they went to the Phoenix school – perhaps, they admitted, the handcuffs described by Zipser were necessary. They knew that some of those so-called students had no intention of learning anything at school. They went to Phoenix "to party, man, to party." [12] Even if stories of abuse were true, tribal councils had other serious problems to deal with, and their children's education was not always their top priority.

Zipser's article finally attracted the attention of the BIA's Central Office in Washington, D.C., which, in 1985, appointed a team of educators to evaluate conditions at the Phoenix school. Team leader Levon French from the Billings Area Office, Joy Martin, Jeanette Smith, and Erna Skye, all from Washington, Bruce Pray from the Aberdeen Area Office, and Dr. Helen Zongolowicz from the Navajo Area Office all descended on Phoenix Indian High School for five days of intensive investigation. They reviewed procedures and interviewed teachers, administrators and support staff before drawing up their recommendations. Their report, dated December 1985, indicated dramatically the failure of the Phoenix school to meet the needs of its students. [13]

Of immediate concern was the lack of direct interaction between teachers and students, who were forced to work almost entirely from workbooks, worksheets, and cassette tapes. Teachers were unable to show individualized lesson plans for the twenty Special Education students, and those involved in that program were poorly trained in testing and evaluation procedures. There was no coordination between the academic, vocational, and residential guidance programs, and few attempts were made to enlist community resources that might enrich the students' learning. In addition, students had mostly unstructured free time from 3:15 to 9:00 PM every day, during which there was little to do. Even the library was closed during those hours. Finally, there was no evidence of, and even considerable resistance to, the idea of parental or tribal involvement in matters involving individual children. When Linda Helser's January 1986 article appeared in the *Arizona Republic*,

Dr. Frank Clarke's bleak statistics underscored an already critical situation. During the following year, an initial enrollment of over five hundred students dropped by approximately two hundred.

Members of the School Board finally began to grasp the reality of what was happening at their school, and in March they recommended to the BIA area office that Richard Christman's contract not be renewed. Area Education Director Pete Soto relieved Christman of his duties at the school and reassigned him to the area office. [14]

By that time, at the invitation of the School Board, the Inter Tribal Council of Arizona had also become involved. It began its own investigation of the evidence in the school's security log and the events that had led to the crisis, and fully supported the Board's demand. The Council's report dated June of that year stated that once again "feelings about the PIHS management were negative, with many weaknesses and very few identified strengths. The management was termed to be ineffective, unorganized, and lacked skills to effectively carry out their duties."

From the students' view, management was "lax, lenient, and ineffective." Poor communication characterized all areas of operation, resulting in a lack of direction, program coordination, and overall planning. The Council recommended hiring a principal "who is recognized for providing strong leadership in a school setting. The individual's philosophy, leadership style, and personality should reflect openness, involvement, planning, visibility, decisiveness, trustworthiness, and humanness." [15]

One might argue cynically, as some did, that if the school was going to close, and it almost certainly was, there was no point in spending a great deal of time and money trying to improve it. The Reagan administration had steadily cut funds for Indian education, and with enrollment sure to drop even more when the new Hopi and Tohono O'odham (Papago) high schools opened, requests for increased funding were sure to be ignored. Those reservations were the last to send large numbers of students to Phoenix, and they would soon be keeping most of their students at home. Students who went to Phoenix would be the ones needing the most help, which the school would not be able to offer. As Zipser flatly stated in his article, "Today, PIHS neither educates nor assimilates; about all that can be said in its favor is that it may be almost extinct." [16]

With this attitude prevailing, it is not surprising that the administrators who succeeded Christman were hardly more than care-takers who accomplished little in the way of educational reform. Enrollment dropped steadily as students and faculty faced uncertainty from one semester to the next about when the school would close. Finally, Milford Sanderson was appointed in March 1988 to do what he could to rescue the school's reputation and to oversee its last years. By that time, only 108 students were enrolled.

Some people have suggested that the city used the troubles at Phoenix Indian School to turn public support against it, that the articles in *New Times* were part of a larger conspiracy to force the closure of the school. While such a conscious attempt to manipulate public opinion seems unlikely, the school's troubles certainly provided ammunition for those who wanted to see the land developed commercially. There had been subdued but continuous talk since 1965 about closing the school, and in 1982, when President Reagan declared his sympathy for the idea, business interests were only too ready to help make it happen. Another *Arizona Republic* columnist, E. J. Montini, observed that the Phoenix Indian School land was "going to be someone's $100 million bonanza – soon." The campus, he pointed out, "is now the largest, best-located, least-developed plot of land remaining in the heart of the city." [17] Developers made certain that the Indian Bureau's Area Director and his staff were aware of their interest.

Since 1982, proposals for future use of the school property had been made by a number of different parties. Some members of the Phoenix City Council hoped that a portion of it, at least, might become available for an urban park. The adjacent Veterans Hospital wanted more parking space, and its administration hoped that one or two of the dormitories might be converted into a veterans' nursing home. Developers, however, would probably be allowed to bid on most of the property. Indian people, who had no economic interest in the land, had little input into the various proposals until late in the discussion, although some of the would-be developers did recognize their concern.

What most of the Indian people wanted, if the high school as such were to be closed, was a facility to provide practical vocational training and competent professional help for their troubled young people. [18] The new reservation high schools did not have the money to provide the facilities needed for training in modern electronics and computers, and while the reservations had been authorized by Public Law 93-638 to contract for delivery of social services, it would be years before they could deal effectively with the mammoth behavioral problems of their young people. If non-Indian communities with much more extensive resources were unable to cope with that problem, how could individual Indian reservations hope to do so? However inadequate the school's response to those problems had been, with it gone, where would such help come from?

In addition to those concerns, Arizona's Indian population and a number of Phoenix residents were also interested in preserving the several old buildings that remained on the campus. Perhaps they could be incorporated into the proposed city park, where they could become the focal point for preserving Indian history and for educating the community about the Indians' on-going contribution to the State of Arizona. The North American Indian Women's Association, whose concern and support had frequently aided the school in the past, continued to be a vocal advocate for preserving the old buildings, and Elsie James, a Hopi woman who had spent most of her life at the school as a student and later as a member of the staff, was one of the leaders in this effort.

After several years of negotiation, a number of these various proposals were incorporated into a Congressional bill that was signed by President Reagan in November 1988. [19] Known as the Arizona-Idaho Conservation Act of 1988, or Public Law 100-696, the act essentially provided for a trade of properties between the Department of the Interior and the multiple Barron-Collier companies of Florida. Pending the satisfaction of technical requirements concerning zoning, bidding procedures, and Interior Department appraisals, the Indian School land was to be divided among the interested parties: sixty-eight percent would be developed by the Barron-Collier interests with the city retaining a significant voice in aesthetic control, eighteen percent would go to the City of Phoenix for an urban park, the Veterans Administration would get ten percent for hospital expansion, and the remaining four percent would revert to the State of Arizona. [20]

In exchange, the National Park Service would receive approximately 115,000 acres of land in Florida owned by the Barron-Collier family. This land, which would become the Florida Panther Wildlife Refuge and the Ten Thousand Islands Wildlife Refuge, would be added to the Big Cypress National Preserve in Florida to protect the Everglades from further environmental degradation. In addition to this Florida acreage, Barron-Collier would contribute $35 million cash for a trust fund for the education of Arizona Indian children in grades one through twelve, most of which would be administered by the Inter Tribal Council of Arizona. The Phoenix school was to be vacated by August 31, 1990.[21]

So a handful of students, forty-four in all, returned to Phoenix Indian High School in the fall of 1989. Many of the teachers and students had already moved elsewhere. The remaining population at the school precariously balanced their lives on almost daily rumors of imminent closure. Although some Congressmen protested the cost of keeping the entire school open for just those few students, the commitment had been made, and there would be a graduating class of 1990. Students prepared the final year book and decorated Memorial Hall for the last Senior Prom.

There was resigned sadness in many of the Indian communities in Arizona when senior citizens talked about their years at Phoenix Indian School. Problems were for the most part forgotten, and childhood memories were shared with smiles and laughter. More recent graduates had other memories that time had not yet dulled, and while they admitted that perhaps it was time for the school to go, they were sad that it had to close under such unhappy circumatances.

Were the citizens of Phoenix sorry to see the school go? The answer is probably no. Arizona's Indian population and the few long-time residents who seemed interested in the old buildings were people who had had some direct contact with the school through parents or grand-parents, or had themselves been students, teachers or members of the staff. While it appears that their efforts to preserve the historic buildings have been successful (they will probably be incorporated into the city park), for the most part the city expressed no regrets. Recent arrivals to the burgeoning metropolitan area did not even know the school was there. As an indication of its indifference, the *Arizona Republic*, which celebrated its one hundredth birthday by publishing a four-section supplement on the city's history in May 1990, never mentioned the school or the role it had played in the community.

But Arizona's Indians knew that they were losing a piece of their collective history. At the school's invitation, the Inter Tribal Council of Arizona helped organize one last Open House during the three days prior to the Thursday graduation. Hundreds of Indian people came from as far away as California and Chicago. They met old classmates, ate fry bread and barbecued beef or picnicked under the trees, and reminisced over a display of old photographs. Children from some of the reservation schools arrived by bus to dance in traditional costumes for the guests or to entertain the crowd with band music, much as their parents and grandparents had done generations earlier. There were speeches about the school's history and about the glory days of its athletic teams. Joe Famulatte, Rita Ventura, Joel Querta, Ivan Sidney, Leonard Haskie, Vincent Little, and Glenn and Myrtle Lundeen renewed old friendships and shared their personal memories.

Finally those last nineteen graduates in their caps and gowns received their diplomas from Principal Milford Sanderson and from their tribal chairmen. Parents and grandparents, brothers and sisters, filled old Memorial Hall, and they wept as the graduates walked slowly down the aisle to the traditional strains of "Pomp and Circumstance." After one last lunch, an Honor Guard played "Taps" and the flag was lowered. Phoenix Indian High School then closed its door on the last group of students from Arizona's Indian tribes. It will be remembered in the minds and hearts of many.

PHOTOGRAPHS

1. Fire Escape
at Casa Saguaro
Dormitory

2. An Unknown Student and His Art – 1930s

3. Agricultural Program – Livestock ,
   left to right: Alonzo Thomas and Harry Domingo

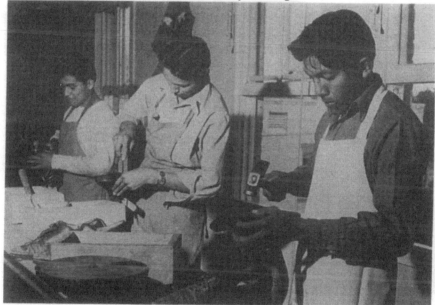

4. Vocational Training – Shoe Repair, left to right:
   Benedict Humetewa, Harold Kazhe, Percy Cannon

5. Senior Picnic, 1946

6. Print Shop, left to right: Hilton Bricker, Oliver Duffina
(Instructer), and Woody Tsosie

7. The Oval – Graduation

8. Nativity Pageant, 1958

9. A Crowded Dining Hall

10. Open House, Westley Hunter and Guests

11 Members of the Dance Group

12 Apache Dancers

13. The New Classroom Buildings, 1965

14. Hitting the Books, left to right: Anita Juan Fred, Vera Swift, and
Francis Begay

15. Senior Prom, left to right: Dollie Hoskie, Vivian Sevecie, and others unknown.

Photographs are courtesy of the National Archives,
Pacific Southwest Region, Laguna Niguel, California.

Appendix A

Service Record, Company F, Arizona National Guard

DEPARTMENT OF THE ARMY

𝕷𝖎𝖓𝖊𝖆𝖌𝖊 𝖆𝖓𝖉 𝕳𝖔𝖓𝖔𝖗𝖘

158th INFANTRY
(Bushmasters)

Organized as the 1st Arizona Volunteer Infantry and mustered into Federal service September - November 1865 by companies (A, B, C, E, F) for one year; mustered out September - November 1866

Reorganized by elements May 1882 - April 1892 as 1st Regiment Infantry, Arizona Militia

(Arizona Militia redesignated 19 March 1891 as Arizona National Guard)

Mustered into Federal service May - June 1916 for service on the Mexican border

Drafted into Federal service 5 August 1917

Reorganized and redesignated 3 October 1917 as 158th Infantry, an element of the 40th Division

Demobilized 3 May 1919 at Camp Kearny, California

Reorganized as 158th Infantry, assigned to the 45th Division, and Federally recognized 12 September 1924 with Headquarters at Phoenix

Inducted into Federal service 16 September 1940 at home stations

Relieved 11 February 1942 from assignment to the 45th Division

Inactivated 17 January 1946 in Japan

Reorganized as 158th Infantry and Federally recognized 18 February 1947 with Headquarters at Tucson

Reorganized 1 March 1959 as 158th Infantry, a parent regiment under the Combat Arms Regimental System, to consist of the 1st and 2d Battle Groups

158th INFANTRY
(Bushmasters)

CAMPAIGN PARTICIPATION CREDIT

Indian Wars
Arizona 1866

World War I
Without inscription

World War II
American Theater without
  inscription
Now Guinea (with arrowhead)
Bismarck Archipelago
Luzon (with arrowhead)

DECORATIONS

Philippine Presidential Unit Citation, Streamer embroidered 17 OCTOBER 1944 TO 4 JULY 1945

Company A (Safford), 2d Battle Group additionally entitled to:

Distinguished Unit Citation, Streamer embroidered LINGAYEN GULF

By Order of the Secretary of the Army:

J. C. LAMBERT
Major General, USA
The Adjutant General

Appendix B

Hall of Fame

In 1977 the Phoenix Indian School established The Hall of Fame to recognize a number of its graduate students for outstanding achievements in leadership, community service, citizenship, and the arts.

Vincent Little, Mojave: 1951

William James, Pima: 1932

Delbridge Honanie, Hopi: 1968

Mary Morez, Navajo: 1960

Ivan L. Sidney, Sr., Hopi: 1966

Elsie Kachinvinsie James, Hopi: 1931

Earl Havatone, Hualapai: 1950

Lucille Jackson–Watahomigie, Hualapai: 1963

Billman Hayes, Pima: 1924

Wintona Winfred Quechan, Hualapai: 1934

Della Sam Williams, Papago: 1956

Clinton M. Pattea, Yavapai: 1954

Peterson Zah, Navajo: 1958

Dollie Lee Yazzie, Navajo: 1954

Logan Koopee, Hopi: 1925

Appendix C

Watermelon Rind Preserves

Cut away the red part of the melon and trim off the tough green outside part, then cut the white into chunks about an inch square or smaller. Soak this overnight in salt water, using one-fourth cup of salt to one quart of water. Next morning, drain and rinse. Measure the rind, and cook in fresh water until tender. Make a syrup, using three-fourths as much sugar as there is of rind, and add half as much water as sugar. Cook until the sugar is dissolved. Drain the water from the cooked rind and add the syrup. Cook until the rind looks clear and transparent. Seal in glass jars until ready to be used. Lemon juice or vinegar, if added, improves the flavor as it adds tartness. Use grated rind and juice of one lemon to about 2 cups of rind. Spices are also sometimes added to the syrup. Allspice, cinnamon, and cloves are good, and may be tied in a small cheesecloth bag, and taken out when the preserves are cooked.

Adapted from *The Phoenix Redskin*, September 22, 1934

Appendix D

Samples of Early Printing in the Navajo Language

From the National Archives, Pacific Southwest Region,
Laguna Niguel, California.
Photograph by Mark O. Rudo, National Park Service.

Development of the "Government" orthography for printing the Little Herder Series.

From the National Archives, Pacific Southwest Region,
Laguna Niguel, California.
Photograph by Mark O. Rudo, National Park Service.

LITTLE HERDER IN WINTER

by

Anna Nolan Clark

Snow

My mother's land is white with snow.
The sandwash and the waterhole,
The dry grass patches and the cornfield
Hide away
Under the white blanket,
Under the snow blanket
That covers the land.

From the National Archives, Pacific Southwest Region,
Laguna Niguel, California.
Photograph by Mark O. Rudo, National Park Service.

The air is filled
With falling snow,
Thick snow,
Soft snow,
Falling,
Falling.

Beautiful mountain
And the red rock canyons
Hide their faces
In snow clouds.

The wind cries.
It piles the snow
In drift banks
Against the poles
Of the sheep corral.
It pushes against the door
Of my mother's hogan,
And it cries,
The wind cries
Out there
In the snow and the cold.

From the National Archives, Pacific Southwest Region,
Laguna Niguel, California.
Photograph by Mark O. Rudo, National Park Service.

Three Navajo posters.

Nahodji god'go nada ya'a'd'e

Only the one who hoes has good corn

Nitsin'na bas bikho'de tse'so Yichi dasi'ago enisin.

Keep a red light on the rear end of your wagon.

Woneh'eh do a'hisdizha da. Kho' bidohidozha.

Don't spit on the ground inside. Spit in the fire.

Selected Pages from Book III Reader, Wycliffe Bible Translators in collaboration with the Summer Institute of Linguistics, Robert W. Young, Specialist in Indian Languages. Illustrated by Andrew Van Tsihnahjinnie.

BOOK III

READER

DINÉ   BIZAAD   WÓLTA'GO
di né   bi zaad   wól ta' go

BEE   BÍHOO'AAHII
bee   bí hoo 'aa hii

TEXT BY
THE WYCLIFFE BIBLE TRANSLATORS IN COLLABORATION WITH
THE SUMMER INSTITUTE OF LINGUISTICS

ILLUSTRATED BY
ANDREW VAN TSIHNAHJINNIE

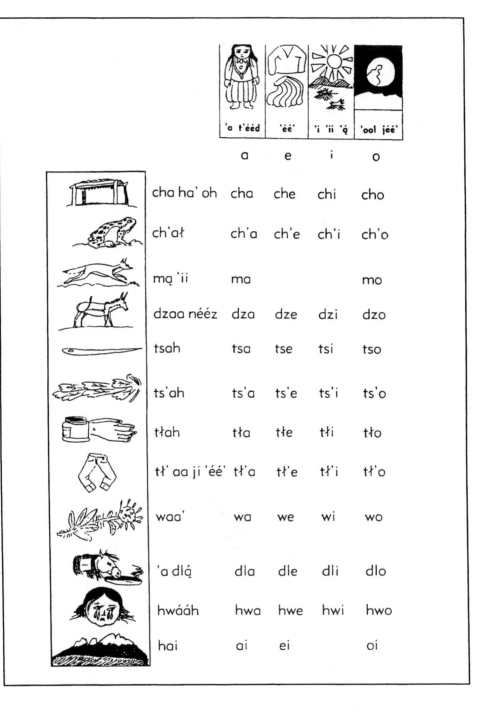

	'a t'ééd	'éé'	'i 'íí 'ǫ́	'ool jéé'
	a	e	i	o
cha ha' oh	cha	che	chi	cho
ch'ał	ch'a	ch'e	ch'i	ch'o
mǫ 'ii	ma			mo
dzaa nééz	dza	dze	dzi	dzo
tsah	tsa	tse	tsi	tso
ts'ah	ts'a	ts'e	ts'i	ts'o
tłah	tła	tłe	tłi	tło
tł' aa ji 'éé'	tł'a	tł'e	tł'i	tł'o
waa'	wa	we	wi	wo
'a dlą́	dla	dle	dli	dlo
hwááh	hwa	hwe	hwi	hwo
hai	ai	ei		oi

Appendix E

Student Poetry from *New Trails,* 1953 Edition

SUMMER WORK

At home in summer
  I help my mother work
  and get her water and wood.
I help cook for my brother
  who works at Sells.

SUSIE MANUEL, Age 13.

IN THE FIELD

In the summer
  we plant watermelons, corn, beans.

On a post in the field
  we hang a cowbell.
We tie a long rope to the bell
  and when we pull the rope
  the bell will say ting-a-ling-a-ling.
  to scare away the birds.

Near the field
  we make a shed to keep us cool
  and when the sun goes down
  rabbits always come around
  and look for food.

When we are hungry
  we get a watermelon
  and eat it under the shed.

STANLEY SCHAFFER, Age 12.

Appendix F

Measured Drawings and Site Plans

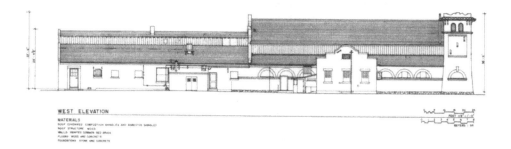

WEST ELEVATION

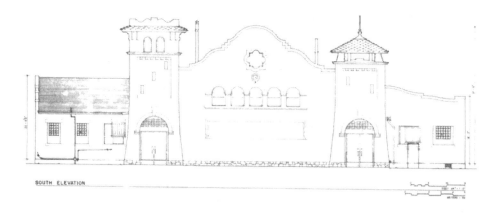

SOUTH ELEVATION

Historic American Building Survey, National Park Service, 1990, AZ-145

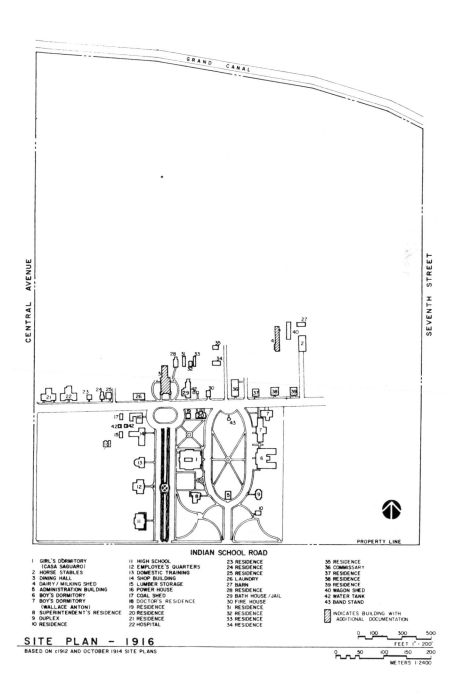

GRAND CANAL

CENTRAL AVENUE

SEVENTH STREET

PROPERTY LINE

INDIAN SCHOOL ROAD

1	GIRL'S DORMITORY (CASA SAGUARO)	11	HIGH SCHOOL	23	RESIDENCE	35	RESIDENCE
2	HORSE STABLES	12	EMPLOYEE'S QUARTERS	24	RESIDENCE	36	COMMISSARY
3	DINING HALL	13	DOMESTIC TRAINING	25	RESIDENCE	37	RESIDENCE
4	DAIRY / MILKING SHED	14	SHOP BUILDING	26	LAUNDRY	38	RESIDENCE
5	ADMINISTRATION BUILDING	15	LUMBER STORAGE	27	BARN	39	RESIDENCE
6	BOY'S DORMITORY	16	POWER HOUSE	28	RESIDENCE	40	WAGON SHED
7	BOY'S DORMITORY (WALLACE ANTON)	17	COAL SHED	29	BATH HOUSE / JAIL	42	WATER TANK
		18	DOCTOR'S RESIDENCE	30	FIRE HOUSE	43	BAND STAND
8	SUPERINTENDENT'S RESIDENCE	19	RESIDENCE	31	RESIDENCE		
9	DUPLEX	20	RESIDENCE	32	RESIDENCE		INDICATES BUILDING WITH ADDITIONAL DOCUMENTATION
10	RESIDENCE	21	RESIDENCE	33	RESIDENCE		
		22	HOSPITAL	34	RESIDENCE		

SITE PLAN - 1916
BASED ON c1912 AND OCTOBER 1914 SITE PLANS

0 100   300   500
FEET 1" = 200'

0   50   100   150   200
METERS 1:2400

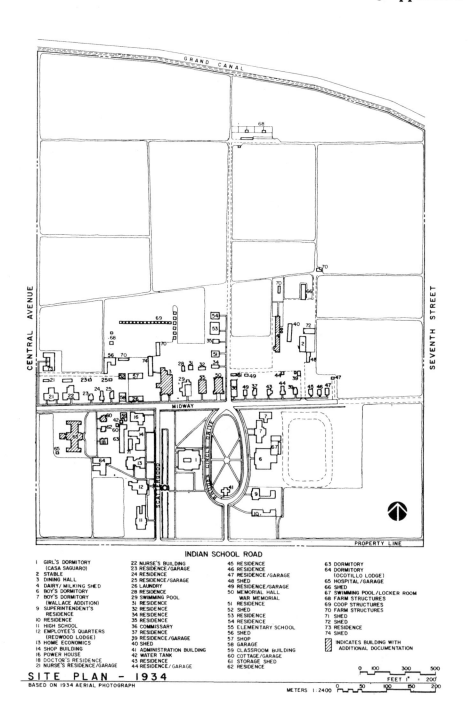

INDIAN SCHOOL ROAD

1 GIRL'S DORMITORY (CASA SAGUARO)	22 NURSE'S BUILDING	45 RESIDENCE	63 DORMITORY
2 STABLE	23 RESIDENCE/GARAGE	46 RESIDENCE	64 DORMITORY (OCOTILLO LODGE)
3 DINING HALL	24 RESIDENCE	47 RESIDENCE/GARAGE	65 HOSPITAL/GARAGE
4 DAIRY/MILKING SHED	25 RESIDENCE/GARAGE	48 SHED	66 SHED
6 BOY'S DORMITORY	26 LAUNDRY	49 RESIDENCE/GARAGE	67 SWIMMING POOL/LOCKER ROOM
7 BOY'S DORMITORY (WALLACE ADDITION)	28 RESIDENCE	50 MEMORIAL HALL WAR MEMORIAL	68 FARM STRUCTURES
9 SUPERINTENDENT'S RESIDENCE	29 SWIMMING POOL	51 RESIDENCE	69 COOP STRUCTURES
	31 RESIDENCE	52 SHED	70 FARM STRUCTURES
10 RESIDENCE	32 RESIDENCE	53 RESIDENCE	71 SHED
11 HIGH SCHOOL	34 RESIDENCE	54 RESIDENCE	72 SHED
12 EMPLOYEE'S QUARTERS (REDWOOD LODGE)	35 RESIDENCE	55 ELEMENTARY SCHOOL	73 RESIDENCE
13 HOME ECONOMICS	36 COMMISSARY	56 SHED	74 SHED
14 SHOP BUILDING	37 RESIDENCE	57 SHOP	
16 POWER HOUSE	39 RESIDENCE/GARAGE	58 GARAGE	
18 DOCTOR'S RESIDENCE	40 SHED	59 CLASSROOM BUILDING	
21 NURSE'S RESIDENCE/GARAGE	41 ADMINISTRATION BUILDING	60 COTTAGE/GARAGE	
	42 WATER TANK	61 STORAGE SHED	
	43 RESIDENCE	62 RESIDENCE	
	44 RESIDENCE/GARAGE		INDICATES BUILDING WITH ADDITIONAL DOCUMENTATION

SITE PLAN - 1934

BASED ON 1934 AERIAL PHOTOGRAPH

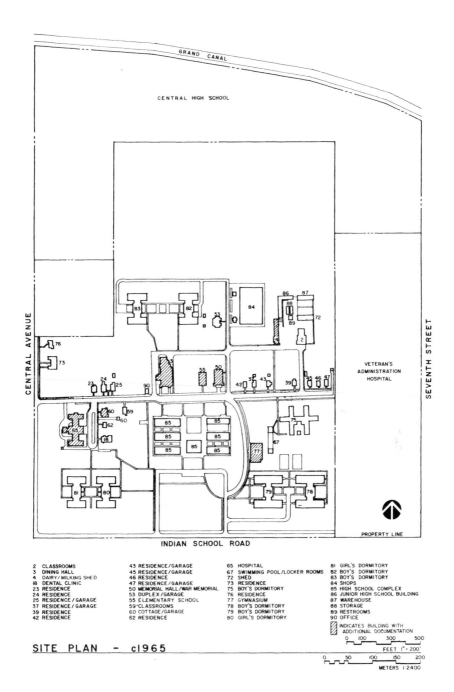

SITE PLAN — c1965

2	CLASSROOMS	43	RESIDENCE/GARAGE	65 HOSPITAL
3	DINING HALL	45	RESIDENCE/GARAGE	67 SWIMMING POOL/LOCKER ROOMS
4	DAIRY/MILKING SHED	46	RESIDENCE	72 SHED
18	DENTAL CLINIC	47	RESIDENCE/GARAGE	73 RESIDENCE
23	RESIDENCE	50	MEMORIAL HALL/WAR MEMORIAL	75 BOY'S DORMITORY
24	RESIDENCE	53	DUPLEX/GARAGE	76 RESIDENCE
25	RESIDENCE/GARAGE	55	ELEMENTARY SCHOOL	77 GYMNASIUM
37	RESIDENCE/GARAGE	59	CLASSROOMS	78 BOY'S DORMITORY
39	RESIDENCE	60	COTTAGE/GARAGE	79 BOY'S DORMITORY
42	RESIDENCE	62	RESIDENCE	80 GIRL'S DORMITORY

81 GIRL'S DORMITORY
82 BOY'S DORMITORY
83 BOY'S DORMITORY
84 SHOPS
85 HIGH SCHOOL COMPLEX
86 JUNIOR HIGH SCHOOL BUILDING
87 WAREHOUSE
88 STORAGE
89 RESTROOMS
90 OFFICE

INDICATES BUILDING WITH ADDITIONAL DOCUMENTATION

0   100   300   500
FEET 1" = 200'

0   50   100   150   200
METERS 1:2400

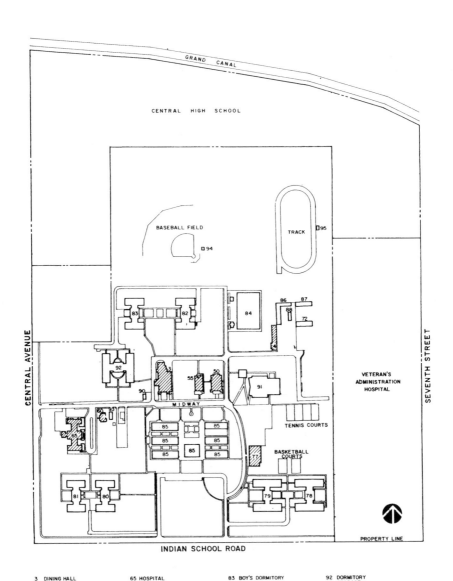

GRAND CANAL

CENTRAL HIGH SCHOOL

CENTRAL AVENUE

SEVENTH STREET

BASEBALL FIELD

TRACK

□95

□94

83

82

84

86   87

88

72

92

55   50

91

VETERAN'S
ADMINISTRATION
HOSPITAL

90

MIDWAY

60

65

85   85

85   85

85   85

TENNIS COURTS

77

BASKETBALL
COURTS

81   80

79   78

PROPERTY LINE

INDIAN SCHOOL ROAD

3 DINING HALL	65 HOSPITAL	83 BOY'S DORMITORY	92 DORMITORY
4 DAIRY/MILKING SHED	72 SHED	84 SHOPS	93 STORAGE
50 MEMORIAL HALL/	77 GYMNASIUM	85 HIGH SCHOOL COMPLEX	94 SHED
WAR MEMORIAL	78 BOY'S DORMITORY	86 JUNIOR HIGH SCHOOL BUILDING	95 STAND
55 ELEMENTARY SCHOOL	79 BOY'S DORMITORY	87 WAREHOUSE	
	80 GIRL'S DORMITORY	88 STORAGE	INDICATES BUILDING WITH
60 COTTAGE	81 GIRL'S DORMITORY	90 STORAGE	ADDITIONAL DOCUMENTATION
	82 BOY'S DORMITORY	91 GYMNASIUM	

SITE PLAN - 1988

BASED ON 1988 AERIAL PHOTOGRAPH

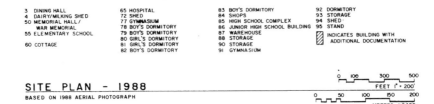

0   100   300   500
FEET 1" = 200'

0   50   100   150   200
METERS 1:2400

SOURCES

Books

Fuchs, Estelle, and Havighurst, Robert J. *To Live on This Earth: American Indian Education*. Albuquerque: University of New Mexico Press, 1972.

Hammerschlag, Carl A. The Dancing Healers: *A Doctor's Journey of Healing with Native Americans.* San Francisco: Harper & Row, 1988.

Lancaster, Roy. *The Story of the Bushmasters,* with a Foreword by Brig. Gen. Hanford MacNider. Detroit: Lancaster Publications, n.d.

Merriam, Lewis, et al. *The Problem of Indian Administration.* Baltimore: Johns Hopkins University Press, 1928.

Shaw, Anna Moore. *A Pima Past.* Tucson: University of Arizona Press, 1974.

Szasz, Margaret Connell. *Education and the American Indian: The Road to Self-Determination Since 1928.* Albuquerque: University of New Mexico Press, 2nd ed., 1977.

Trennert, Robert. *The Phoenix Indian School: Forced Assimilation in Arizona, 1891-1935.* Norman: University of Oklahoma Press, 1988.

Articles

Hammerschlag, Carl A., M.D.; Alderfer, Ph.D.; and Berg, David, M.A. "Indian Education: A Human Systems Analysis." *American Journal of Psychiatry* 130 (October 1973): 1098-1102.

Littlefield, Alice. "The B.I.A. Boarding School: Theories of Resistance and Social Reproduction." *Humanity and Society* 13 (1989): 428-441.

Trennert, Robert A. "Corporal Punishment and the Politics of Indian Reform." *History of Education Quarterly* 29 (Winter 1989): 595-617.

Newspapers

Arizona Republic
Indians at Work
Native American
New Times
The Redskin, aka *The Phoenix Redskin*

Unpublished Material

Arizona Historical Foundation Archives, Hayden Library, Arizona State
       University, Tempe, Arizona. "Progress Report of 1952-53," prepared by
       Glenn Lundeen.

Arizona Historical Foundation Archives, Hayden Library, Arizona State
       University, Tempe, Arizona. "Phoenix Indian High School
       Reevaluation, 1966."

Bureau of Indian Affairs, Central Office, Indian Education Programs. "Team
       Evaluation, Phoenix Indian School." December 1985. Office of Inter
       Tribal Council of Arizona, Phoenix.

Inter Tribal Council of Arizona, Phoenix. "Management Review, Phoenix
       Indian High School." Prepared for the Phoenix Indian High School
       Board, June 1986.

NOTES

Introduction

1 Robert Trennert, *The Phoenix Indian School: Forced Assimilation in Arizona,* 1891-1935 (Norman: University of Oklahoma, 1988). This work traces the school's early years and contrasts federal Indian policy with local reality in the development of relations between the City of Phoenix and the Indian School.

2 Lewis Merriam et al, *The Problem of Indian Administration* (Baltimore: Johns Hopkins Press, 1928).

3 Trennert, *Phoenix Indian School,* p. 182. See Note 1 above.

4 Ibid., pp. 29-31.

5 Ibid., p. 19.

Chapter One

1 Trennert, *Phoenix Indian School,* pp. 187-195. See also, Robert Trennert, "Corporal Punishment and the Politics of Reform," *History of Education Quarterly* 29(Winter 1989):595-617.

2 Trennert, "Corporal Punishment," p. 617.

3 Alice Littlefield, "The B.I.A. Boarding School: Theories of Resistance and Social Reproduction," *Humanity and Society* 13(1989):435.

4 Katie Pierson, the wife of an instructor at Phoenix Indian School in the 1950s, wrote an informal history of the school and included this bit of information. Her study, "History of Phoenix Indian School," was not published. A copy may be found in the Arizona Collection, Hayden Library, Arizona State University, Tempe, Arizona, hereafter cited as Ariz. Coll., HL.

5 Paul Coze File, Heard Museum Library, Phoenix, Arizona.

6 *Native American,* November 15, 1924, Ariz. Coll., HL.

7 Ibid.

8 *The Phoenix Redskin,* November 11, 1933, Ariz. Coll., HL. The Arizona Collection has an incomplete run of the student newspaper from 1931 to the 1980s.

9 Box 3, Records of the State Supervisor of Education, Agricultural Reports for 1938-1939, 1939-1940. Phoenix Indian School, Record Group 75, Records of the BIA, National Archives, Pacific Southwest Region, Laguna Niguel, California. Hereafter cited as RG 75, Laguna Niguel.

10 Box 2/2, 1938-1939 Agriculture Office, CCC-ID Office Files 1936-47, Phoenix Indian School, RG 75, Laguna Niguel.

11 Library Bus, #751, Central Classified Files, Phoenix Indian School, RG 75, Laguna Niguel.

12 *The Phoenix Redskin*, September 22, 1934, Ariz. Coll., HL.

13 Box 2/2, 1938-1939 Agriculture Office, CCC-ID Office Files 1936-1947, RG, Laguna Niguel.

14 Navajo translations found in Box 1, English and Navajo Manuscripts, "Little Herder in Winter," mistakenly labeled "Poems 1940." Phoenix Indian School, RG 75, Laguna Niguel.

15 Margaret Connell Szasz, *Education and the American Indian: The Road to Self-Determination Since 1928* (Albuquerque: University of New Mexico, 2nd ed., 1977), pp. 73-4.

16 Personal interview, Lloyd Henry New, April 28, 1990, Santa Fe, New Mexico.

17 Personal Interview, Robert W. Young, April 27, 1990, Albuquerque, New Mexico.

Chapter Two

1 Anna Moore Shaw, *A Pima Past* (Tucson: University of Arizona, 1974), pp. 146.

2 Ibid.

3 *Native American*, July 12, 1924, pp. 150-51; Roy Lancaster, *The Story of the Bushmasters, with a Foreword by Brig. Gen. Hanford MacNider* (Detroit: Lancaster Publishers, n.d.). Information about the Bushmasters was also obtained from the Arizona National Guard Museum, Phoenix, courtesy Col. John Johnson.

4 Agricultural production was tremendous. Estimates for 1940 include 380,000 lbs. of whole milk, 33,500 lbs. of pork, 25,000 lbs. of fresh vegetables, 6,500 dozen eggs, and 1,000 chickens; 168 head of sheep and 10 yearling steers were slaughtered; 32,700 lbs. of barley and 160 tons of feed were harvested. Statistics from 1939-1940 Agricultural Report of the Phoenix Indian School, Records of the State Supervisor of Indian Education - 1931-43, RG 75, Laguna Niguel.

5 Glenn Lundeen provided the author with BIA literature on the Special Navajo Program, and Beverly Queal, who ran the program at Phoenix Indian School, provided other details. For the significance of the program in Indian education, see Szasz, *Education and the American Indian,* pp. 116-20, and Estelle Fuchs and Robert J. Havighurst, *To Live on this Earth: American Indian Education* (Albuquerque: University of New Mexico, 1972), pp. 227-28. Chapter 11, "Boarding Schools," is especially pertinent.

6 The original wooden flagpole was quite obviously a ship's mast, the origin of which has since been lost.

7 Ibid., pp. 134-40.

8 "Progress Report of 1952-53," prepared by Glenn Lundeen, Arizona Historical Foundation Archives, Hayden Library, Arizona State University, Tempe, Arizona.

9 The program for the Knickerball Ball was loaned to the author by Glenn Lundeen from his personal papers.

10 Press Release received by the BIA on October 15, 1957, from the Arizona Knickerbocker Ball Committee. Copy from the personal papers of Glenn Lundeen.

11 Szasz, *Education and the American Indian*, p. 154.

12 Quoted in *The Redskin*, January 28,1955, from the *Arizona Republic.*

Chapter Three

1 Fuchs and Havighurst, *To Live on This Earth*, Chapter 10, "The School Curriculum," pp. 205-221.

2 "Phoenix Indian High School Reevaluation, 1966," Arizona Historical Foundation, Hayden Library, Arizona State University, Tempe, AZ.

3 Carl A. Hammerschlag, M.D., Clayton P. Alderfer, Ph.D., David Berg, M.A., "Indian Education: A Human Systems Analysis," *American Journal of Psychiatry* 130 (October 1973): 1098-1102. See also, Carl A. Hammerschlag, *The Dancing Healers: A Doctor's Journey of Healing with Native Americans* (San Francisco: Harper & Row, 1988).

4 Szasz, *Education and the American Indian,* pp. 148-51.

5 Ibid., pp. 200-01.

6 *Arizona Republic,* January 3, 1986.

7 Tom Kuhn, "Phoenix Indian School: The End of the Rope," *New Times,* January 2, 1980.

8 *The Redskin,* January 18, 1980.

9 Andy Zipser, "Handcuffs and Too Little Hope, Atypical Education at The Phoenix Indian School," *New Times,* November 28, 1984.

10 *Arizona Republic,* April 26, 1986.   Phyllis Gillespie By-line.

11 Zipser, *New Times,* November 28, 1984.

12 Ibid.

13 "Team Evaluation, Phoenix Indian School," December 1985, prepared on order for Central Office, Indian Education Programs, Bureau of Indian Affairs. Unpublished report, copy in office of Inter Tribal Council of Arizona, Phoenix.

14 *Arizona Republic*, April 26, 1986.

15 "Management Review, Phoenix Indian High School," prepared for Phoenix Indian High School Board by the Inter Tribal Council oif Arizona, Inc., June 1986, pp. 3, 11.

16 Zipser, *New Times,* November 28, 1984.

17 *Arizona Republic*, Column by E. J. Montini, February 5, 1986.

18 *Arizona Republic*, November 20, 1986.

19 "Arizona-Idaho Conservation Act of 1988," or "Public Law 100-696."

20 *Arizona Republic*, October 4, 1988.

21 Ibid.

About the Author

Dorothy R. Parker holds a Ph.D. in history from the University of New Mexico and is an assistant professor emerita at Eastern New Mexico University. She wrote *Phoenix Indian School: The Second Half-Century* while a research assistant at Arizona State University. She is also the author of essays in a number of other books and of *Singing an Indian Song: A Biography of D'Arcy McNickle*.